No Man
Is an Island

No Man Is an Island

COMMUNITY AND COMMEMORATION
ON NORWAY'S UTØYA

JØRGEN WATNE FRYDNES

TRANSLATED BY WENDY H. GABRIELSEN

UNIVERSITY OF MASSACHUSETTS PRESS
AMHERST AND BOSTON

Copyright © 2025 by University of Massachusetts Press
All rights reserved
Printed in the United States of America

ISBN 978-1-62534-848-7 (paper); 849-4 (hardcover)

Designed by Jen Jackowitz
Set in Adobe Jenson Pro by Jen Jackowitz
Printed and bound by Books International, Inc.

Cover design by adam b. bohannon
Cover photo by Lars Petter Pettersen, Utoya Meeting Place. Courtesy of the photographer and Utøya.

Library of Congress Cataloging-in-Publication Data
A catalog record for this book is available from the Library of Congress.

British Library Cataloguing-in-Publication Data
A catalog record for this book is available from the British Library.

Contents

Preface ix

AUTUMN

The first year 8

A small island of huge importance 14

The highlight of the summer—and hell on earth 29

Hate must never win 34

Two formidable tasks 36

Sanding walls and thinking of others 38

WINTER

Difficult phone calls 48

Traumas and inconsolable grief 53

No experience of dealing with terrorism 61

I can't do this anymore 69

Commemoration, learning, and engagement 77

My travels up north 80

Conflicting wishes, impossible choices 85

SPRING

Resistance from the local Progress Party 98

Protecting what is most important 102

Utøya rises from the ashes 112

The memorial on the island: the Clearing 116

The national memorial 126

The importance of the national support group 132

SUMMER

The AUF comes home 139

Hegnhuset is finally built 146

Unfiltered sources 152

One of the most important new buildings in the world 155

How do you commemorate a life? 158

Building a workshop for democracy 162

Epilogue 173

Acknowledgments 185

No man is an island entire of itself; every man
is a piece of the continent, a part of the main;
if a clod be washed away by the sea, Europe
is the less, as well as if a promontory were, as
well as any manner of thy friends or of thine
own were; any man's death diminishes me,
because I am involved in mankind.
And therefore never send to know for whom
the bell tolls; it tolls for thee.

John Donne

Preface

Northern lights, welfare, the more desolate of the Scandinavian countries, a peace prize. On a rainy afternoon in 2011, the international depiction of Norway came to include a new, uncanny association: one of modern history's deadliest right-wing terror attacks. The bombing in Oslo's government quarter and the mass shooting of political youth on the island of Utøya on July 22, 2011, shook both Norway and the world. Seventy-seven people were killed, with the majority being young people and children gathered at a political summer camp.

While the brutal attack itself immediately made global headlines, it was Norway's response that made a lasting impact worldwide in its divergence from the rhetoric of retaliation that since 9/11 had become the standard answer to terror. That same evening, before the perpetrator's motivation or profile was known, Prime Minister Jens Stoltenberg proclaimed that Norway's values would not budge in the face of terror: "The answer to violence is even more democracy. Even more humanity. But never naïveté." In the following days, the Norwegian public took to the streets with roses rather than demands of revenge, and later, the ordinary nature of the court case against the terrorist was met with admiration from international observers.

However, the trauma of terror certainly carried with it anger, discord, and conflict in the Norwegian context as well, not least with regards to the difficult task of memorializing. The small island of Utøya soon became the locus of the small nation's postterror debate. From being a secluded political arena, known to most Norwegians for being where the Workers' Youth League (AUF) ran its summer camp on passion and volunteer work, it became the focal point of national discussion.

The AUF summer camp has a long and strong position in Norwegian political life. Ever since Utøya was given to the AUF by the Norwegian Confederation of Trade Unions in 1950, its story became that of a small island with great political impact. Every summer, generations of labor youth have gathered at Utøya to study, develop, and discuss practical answers to central social questions. Some of them have changed the course of history by affecting the quality of life and living conditions for the Norwegian population. As the Norwegian Labor Party was the country's leading party during the second half of the last century, Utøya and the AUF summer camp have been an arena where influential party figures, ministers, and state leaders have changed their minds, shared visions, and launched reforms. At the same time, it has been a place where future generations of political leaders have been fostered, inspired, and formed.

But most of all, Utøya and the summer camp are known as a unique arena for political youth on the left in Norway, with their rare combination of activism, leisure, and recreation. Through the history of the camps, Utøya has promoted principles of engagement, internationalism and solidarity, diversity and tolerance, and, not least of all, the value of democratic culture, all ideals that were brutally targeted on July 22, 2011.

On July 22, 2011, a thirty-two-year-old ethnonationalist extremist named Anders Behring Breivik detonated a car bomb in the government quarter in Norway's capital of Oslo, killing eight people in or near the building that houses the prime minister's office. As police forces and soldiers in the wake of the explosion rushed to other official buildings to prepare for a potential second attack, the thirty-two-year-old self-proclaimed crusader had his eyes on a different target—the AUF summer camp at Utøya.

Dressed as a policeman, the terrorist reached the Tyrifjord lake around five o'clock in the afternoon. Claiming to be on a mission to secure the island after the explosion in Oslo, he requested to be taken to Utøya by boat, and the island's daily manager Monica Bosei, to many known as "Mother Utøya," joined the alleged police officer on the ferry MS *Thorbjørn* over to the island. On the way, she made sure to cover his weapons case with plastic bags, as she was afraid the firearms would scare the teens who were already upset after the news from Oslo. Upon arrival at Utøya, Bosei and Trond Berntsen, a real policeman volunteering at the camp, confronted Breivik, asking for his ID. They were the first two to be killed, shot dead near the stairs of Utøya's main building. What followed was the deadliest attack in Norway in peacetime.

When the terrorist set foot on the island at 5:17 p.m., 564 people were gathered there, most of them teens and young AUF members attending camp. Although there was nothing random in them being targeted as a collective, survival for each and every one was a matter of chance.

The massacre lasted for seventy-two minutes; 297 shots were fired, a majority at point blank range. A total of sixty-nine people were killed, and another thirty-three seriously injured. Kids hid in restrooms, under rocks, and in the water. They fled barefoot, in the rain, on dirt roads and along the small island's rock-strewn shore; many jumped in the freezing lake, and others jumped out of windows. Many never saw the terrorist, thinking there were several attackers, maybe the onset of war; others noticed his uniform, believing the attack was part of a state coup. Others again had no time to reflect on what happened. Some escaped the bullets, others did not.

Breivik was arrested by special police forces at 6:34 p.m. By then, he had killed a total of seventy-seven people and forever changed the lives of thousands. According to the July 22 support group, one in four Norwegians knows someone who was directly affected by the attack.

In 2012, the terrorist was sentenced to twenty-one years of preventive detention, an indefinite sentence and the maximum punishment in Norway. He admitted carrying out the attacks, although denying criminal guilt—claiming the defense of necessity. Although at his arrest on July 22 the terrorist said he was commander of the so-called Knights Templar Order, and part of a network of European militant nationalists, the court found no evidence such a network ever existed. He planned and executed the terror attack alone. However, the many right-wing attacks executed by so-called lone wolves since 2011 and their referencing of each other through symbols and manifestos show how they are not ideologically lonely— wolves run in packs.

As many terrorists before and after 2011, Breivik proclaimed virtuous arguments for his heinous acts. His ideology is characterized by a mix of Islamophobic, antifeminist, and antidemocratic views, centered around the conspiracy theory of "Eurabia." His so-called manifesto, sent to over one thousand recipients in Norway and abroad ninety minutes before the bomb went off, is filled with hatred toward immigrants, women, the media, and what he calls multiculturalist propaganda. Little of its content is written by the terrorist himself; it mostly consists of texts from other right-wing writers, predominantly operating online. What these agree on, in broad terms, is that Europe is threatened by Muslim immigration and that national "elites" collaborate with Arab countries to increase immigration with the goal of transforming Europe into an "Islamic colony." According to Breivik, the 2011 attacks had to take place to protect Norway against the "deconstruction" of Norwegian ethnicity and culture.

With this ideological backdrop, the decision to set off a bomb in the government quarter is perhaps easier to understand than targeting a summer camp for teens. But in a Norwegian context, the Labor Party is the conspiracy theory's primary "inner enemy," having been in power most of the period during which the politics of liberalism and diversity were implemented. And while the high-rise building in the government quarter was a potent symbol of state power as well as home to the office of the Labor Party's prime minister, Utøya had been raising promising Labor Party prime ministers for years. In fact, prime minister at the time Jens Stoltenberg spent his youth at the island's summer camps. In targeting Utøya, the terrorist sought to "choke future recruitment to the party."

Although the terrorist caused inexplicable harm, he did not succeed in his aims to alter Utøya's position as an important place for youth engagement. Rather, the island has become increasingly important to even more groups of youth all year round. Getting there, however, was neither easy nor a given.

This book is about the dilemmas, discussions, and deliberations that arose in the handling of Utøya after the terrorist attack of July 22, 2011. Norway, fortunately, had no previous history of similar events from which we could learn, so we had to find our own path and our own answers. To a large extent, what we have managed to achieve stems from the difficult, painful, but positive dialogue we have had. We have listened, we have learned, and we have changed direction along the way. Talking together helps. We have had to be pragmatic in order to create a satisfactory whole based on thousands of people's ideas and needs and to be able to accommodate both present and future generations. Thanks to the confidence people have shown us, we have accomplished what many thought was impossible.

Hundreds of people come to Utøya each year to learn from the process that has taken place since 2011: researchers from all over the world, crisis teams, emergency preparedness authorities, academics, and politicians, to name but a few. International experts have described our work and way of thinking as the new gold standard. "I didn't think it was possible to achieve such high ambitions," said Cliff Chanin, vice president of the 9/11 Memorial and Museum in New York to the national newspaper *Aftenposten* during a visit by an American and French delegation. The decisions we have made on Utøya may seem logical to many people today, but that certainly doesn't mean we have come up with the solution for how to manage all places that have been subjected to violence. Our decisions only make sense when seen in light of the background for the attack, as well as the history of Utøya, the AUF, the labor movement, and Norway. Other factors would play the same important role for other places. There is no standard answer, yet there are still lessons to be learned.

How do we commemorate loss and how do we deal with grief? How can we create new life in a charged landscape—without destroying the traces of history? How do we reconcile various and at times completely contradictory opinions and interests? How do we deal with different perceptions of time? How can we create something meaningful out of something meaningless? How do we develop an engaging center of learning where the younger generation can not only find out about July 22 but also look to the future and focus on how they can help to create a tolerant and inclusive society themselves? This book will show how we have responded to these and many other questions on Utøya over the last ten years.

This is my story of what it has been like to have Utøya as a workplace for the twelve years following the terrorist attack. It's a book about Utøya, pain and resilience, the value of talking together, grief and love, life and death.

No Man
Is an Island

AUTUMN

It's Monday, August 1, 2011. My phone rings. On the other end is Pia Gulbrandsen, the Norwegian Labor Party's head of communications. She says that they have put together a small group of people who will be responsible for coordinating, fundraising, and a lot of other matters to do with Utøya after the terrorist attack.

"We need someone that can handle the fundraising for Utøya and all that sort of thing. We've heard you've got the relevant experience and can be here at short notice. Can you help us out?"

Straight to the point. No time to lose.

"Er . . . well, yes, I suppose so."

Did I have a choice? I had no background with the AUF, the Labor Party, or the labor movement. At the same time, and like very many others in Norway, I felt I too was somehow affected. Of course I had to help out.

"Can you come down to our offices for a chat right now?"

"I'm actually nearby, but I'd rather go home and change first. I can be there in an hour?"

"No need to change, just come straight away."

In tatty shorts and a grubby T-shirt after a hike in the forest, I set off on my bike in the direction of Youngstorget, a square in central Oslo. Although my outfit didn't exactly inspire confidence, I understood from Pia that it was important to get started as quickly as possible.

In the few minutes it took to cycle down to Youngstorget, I tried to prepare myself; it was a kind of job interview I was going to, after all. I had been involved in fundraising, communications, and project management for several years, but always for the benefit of people in distant lands. For the last eight years I had worked for Médecins Sans Frontières (MSF), a unique organization with dedicated field workers. Both with them and on my own travels, I had experienced terrible conditions in countries such as Somaliland, Sudan, Sierra Leone, Colombia, Tajikistan, and Congo. The job concerned people in need living in totally different countries and societies than my own. Now terror had struck Norway, and I was going to the heart of the organizations targeted by the attack: the AUF and Labor Party offices at Youngstorget.

On the way there I cycled past the bombed-out government building complex.

On the fifth floor of the People's Theater building, the home of the Labor Party, I met Pia. Most people with an interest in politics would think it would be exciting to be here; you can sense the history and power in the walls. But there was no time for a guided tour. We sat down in a meeting room with Martin Henriksen, chair of Utøya and former AUF leader. After a short conversation I was asked to write a press release about how people could help to rebuild Utøya and also to design a website. Was this a test, or were they just so desperate to get started immediately? Maybe both things at once. I got down to work that very evening.

Like most people in Norway, I was deeply affected by the attack on the government buildings and Utøya on July 22, 2011, but I wasn't affected directly. I was close by, yet also a long way off. My girlfriend, Mona, and I were driving from Oslo to our cabin in Hardangervidda. As we passed Sollihøgda, I got a call from a friend who said that there had been a big explosion in the center of Oslo. We turned on the radio. The tunnel on the motorway was closed, so all traffic had to go past the shores of Utstranda. We drove past Utøya without really noticing it; it was just an island we passed along the edge of the water. All our attention was centered on the dramatic news coming from Oslo. We drove past Hønefoss on to Nesbyen, Flå, and Gol. Then the news shifted focus. There were reports of shootings on Utøya.

Altogether seventy-seven were killed in the attacks, most of them teenagers. The nation was in mourning, and hundreds of thousands of people joined processions, holding roses. When we finally returned to Oslo, the city had already taken its first small steps toward recovery after the bomb attack. The sun was shining but the questions kept churning in the back of people's minds. How was it possible? How are we going to handle this? What can *I* do?

Those who were the target of all this hate—the AUF and the Labor Party—showed us the way forward. Prime Minister Jens Stoltenberg pledged "more openness, more democracy. . . . But never naïveté." Something more concrete, and which would be crucial for my own future, was the AUF's decision to "reclaim Utøya."

"It's essential for everything we believe in that we reopen Utøya," said AUF leader Eskil Pedersen when he stood in Youngstorget on July 26 and launched a fundraising drive for Utøya. The support was massive. Children sold their toys at bazaars and donated the money to the restoration of Utøya. A forest owner in Wales wanted to donate a large oak tree, as a token of the UK's sympathy. Many companies wanted to contribute by offering their services free of charge. The rapper 50 Cent arranged a concert. The trade union movement organized huge fundraisers and promised financial backing, artists donated paintings, and hundreds of ordinary people started their own fundraising schemes. It was all to rebuild Utøya.

I had experience with a lot of this from Médecins Sans Frontières: communications, fundraising, coordinating. It had never been on such a massive scale, however, and I had never been so alone. I was given an office on the fourth floor with the Labor Party. The windowpane had been shattered by the blast in the government quarter, so there was no view to speak of. Very few of the Labor Party's offices at Youngstorget had windows during these months, just chipboard. The working group consisted of Pia Engebretsen, the Labor Party's head of communications; Martin Henriksen, chair of Utøya AS; Kaare Øystein Trædal; and me. Kaare Øystein was probably the reason I was there. He was in charge of the company that hosted the Labor Party's website, a company I had worked with in my previous job at MSF. He was now helping to set up the technical solutions we needed for communications, fundraising, and so on. It was Kaare Øystein that had recommended me.

The big party apparatus had completely different things to attend to than the practical handling of the first phase of reopening Utøya. Looking after all those affected came first. Martin took over responsibility for

Utøya, since he was chair of the company that manages and runs the island. He made the point that the AUF itself shouldn't be burdened with this at the time. Martin was my closest sparring partner, good to talk to when I needed a chat, but he didn't participate in the day-to-day operations. So there I sat, alone in an office at Youngstorget, behind a boarded-up window.

My job in the beginning was to raise money to rebuild Utøya. But what specifically were we raising money for? No one except the police had been to the island since the attack, and we didn't know if the buildings or infrastructure had suffered major material damage. One thing Martin was quite clear about, however, was that whatever the extent of the material damage on the island, the damage done to people's hearts was enormous: "The AUF's goal is to ensure that Utøya remains a place where young people can get together and discuss politics. And to achieve this, the island needs a makeover—to become nicer and better than ever before. There will be many matters to take into account, and it's important that we have the biggest budget possible to make it all happen."

By the middle of August we had already raised over 32 million kroner. All the contributions from children made the deepest impression. Some sold cupcakes, some their baseball caps. Others arranged bazaars, magic shows, and dance performances—it was all to raise money for Utøya.

There also came thousands of external project proposals after July 22. Which should we support? Which initiatives did we believe in, and which did we not want to be directly associated with? It's not unusual that motivated people in times of crisis (national as well as international) want to help by initiating good fundraising projects, which in the end are barely profitable. A plumbing firm that suddenly wanted to produce wristbands and donate the profits was an example of this. Various companies wanted to give us a percentage of their sales, which would obviously be boosted by our logo and support. But was it primarily the individual firm that would gain from this, while Utøya was thrown a few crumbs? There was a lot to consider in just a short time. I received invaluable assistance from a friend and former colleague at MSF. We luckily made the right choices and avoided collaborating on any questionable projects. Utøya received millions of kroner in profits from the best-selling CD that year. The same applied to two major book projects.

People were eager to donate. One example was all the money collected in connection with the rose processions that were held. Municipalities over the whole country sent one krone per inhabitant. However, Norwegian law states that political parties cannot receive gifts from government institutions or accept gifts without knowing who gave them. Even though the AUF wasn't going to spend the contributions on party political work but to rebuild Utøya, it still owned the island and was therefore subject to the provisions of the law regulating how political parties are financed. After a long dialogue with the committee in charge of these matters, it was decided that Utøya could keep gifts sent from abroad, but only from those who explicitly declared that the purpose of the gift was to rebuild Utøya. All other foreign gifts, as well as all those given by municipalities and government organizations in Norway, therefore had to be returned.

Slowly but surely the job of "reclaiming Utøya" got underway. As the work progressed, however, I was about to head off somewhere else entirely. Earlier that year I had been accepted to do an MA in International Relations at the University of York, and term had started some time ago. Should I drop my studies? Mona had resigned from her job to be able to join me there, so it wasn't easy to cancel our plans. I told Martin Henriksen that they would have to find someone else to handle the process from now on. Although it was sad to finish so soon, it actually felt like I had just had a temporary placement in a rather unfamiliar organization. I wished Utøya the best of luck and set off for England.

The first year

There's something terribly brutal about the way life has just continued for the rest of us. The relentless daily grind. There are other news stories to follow, TV programs to watch, books to read, and meals to be made. Insignificant actions that have to be repeated. There hasn't been room for 7/22 anymore. Not in that way. Humans can't manage to stay in the darkest of places for long, so hopefully it's also a good thing that we "forget." Perhaps it's precisely because we are made like this that we manage to move on? Because our brain overrules our conscience and forces us to. But next week we won't have a choice. Now we have to go back in there again. Into the darkest of places. My conscience tells me that it might be about time, too.

—Kristopher Schau, Notes from the July 22 trial,
Oslo District Court, 2012.

I followed the news back home from my student life in England that year. On April 16, 2012, the doors of courtroom 250 opened in Oslo District Court. The coverage was huge, even in the UK. Buried under piles of books, reading lists, and articles about international relations in the university library, it was the trial that took most of my attention. Hundreds of journalists from Norway and abroad tried to put into words what they saw and heard.

The defendant is of the opinion that ethnic Norwegians have been under attack in the form of ethnic "deconstruction" since the Labor Party allowed for mass immigration in the 1960s.

According to the perpetrator, Norway has been transformed into a multicultural state, where the indigenous Norwegian population is in the process of being exterminated. All the parties in Parliament [Storting], but particularly the Labor Party, are responsible for this.

According to the defendant, leading Norwegian politicians are participating in a cooperation with European elites where the aim is to promote "multiculturalism."

Utøya was chosen, inter alia, because the participants at the summer camp were "political activists" from the Labor Party's youth organization and consequently, according to the defendant, "legitimate targets."

The atrocities are unparalleled in Norwegian history.

Terje Emberland, researcher at the Norwegian Center for Holocaust and Minority Studies, said that the perpetrator represented "a kind of modern variety, a modern version of fascism." Tore Bjørgo, specialist in terrorism and racist violence at the Norwegian Police University College, explained that the defendant's talk of a civil war in Europe was a common perception of reality among right-wing extremists.

Even though the political aspect was highlighted, it wasn't *that* that I remember from the trial. The main discussion focused on psychiatric diagnoses rather than right-wing extremism. Did you have to be mad to carry out such an evil act? A Pakistani friend that I studied with asked me if I thought that the Norwegian justice system would in that case call thousands of members of the Taliban mad in his own country, and therefore criminally insane. "You're simply not used to such evil but believe me, it's unfortunately just part of human nature," he said.

Amid all the attention given to the perpetrator's understanding of the world, amid all the cold, clinical words uttered by forensic technicians, amid the academic jargon used by expert witnesses, there also came expressions of humanity from the courtroom. And these simple words were perhaps the most difficult of all to read and hear.

He was looking forward to turning eighteen.

Music meant a lot to him, and he played in a marching band for many years.

She was sociable and outgoing, a real ray of sunshine and a colorful character.

A short eulogy was read aloud for each of the victims in connection with the autopsy reports. Beautiful words, painful words. Words that would become part of my daily life for many years to come. Words about people I would never meet, but that I would come to know well all the same.

He was passionate about societal issues; he felt strongly about things and wasn't afraid to stand up for his opinions. He had a lot a plans for the future and was about to become an uncle.

She was a beautiful girl with so much love for other people. She had a fundamental belief in human kindness. She always showed respect for others and was intrinsically honest.

In the middle of the trial came the first anniversary of the massacre. I sat watching the TV coverage of July 22, 2012. How did the AUF choose to mark the events one year later? Over fifteen hundred people visited Utøya that day. Those of us who followed from a distance, through TV programs and on social media, understood that it was a moving occasion with songs, solidarity, and a clear political profile. Jens Stoltenberg, former prime minister Gro Harlem Brundtland, and Denmark's prime minister Helle Thorning-Smith all took part. Renate Tårnes gave a powerful performance of Kaizer Orchestra's "Hjerteknuser" (Heartbreaker) just 150 meters from where she had witnessed the murder of her boyfriend, Snorre Haller, one year earlier. AUF leader Eskil Pedersen made a fine speech.

> Dear friends. Dear AUF members. On such a painful day, it is good to be together. A year ago today we were sitting together on this hillside at the summer camp that we had been so looking forward to. But there is no summer camp this year. We are here to remember our sixty-nine friends who lost their lives to the perpetrator's incomprehensible evil. And to show that we still stand firm, despite the heavy burden that we bear. Everything changed a year ago. That Friday last summer when it never stopped raining changed the lives of everyone who lost a loved one. It changed the lives of those of us who survived. It changed the AUF. The most beautiful, most innocent thing of all: young people gathered

together at a summer camp to make a difference. To make new friends, to play soccer, to learn. They became victims of an evil we could never have imagined. I am so sorry that this happened to us. I am so sorry that you had to go through this. None of us were meant to encounter such evil. Not you. Not me. We are here today all the same. Back on Utøya, one year later. We are taking important steps to move on in our lives. We all go at a different pace. Sometimes we fall behind. But we keep going. We help each other. And we are here today. And you should know that I am incredibly proud of you all.

The papers wrote about the bereaved, calling it a worthy commemoration, a day filled with reflection and dignity. "It might sound strange to use the word 'nice' about a day like this, but it was a nice day."

In actual fact, there wasn't as much solidarity as there might have seemed from the outside. The AUF had really wanted to hold a political commemoration. The day was to be more than a memorial service; AUF members wanted a gathering where they could make it clear to themselves that it was possible to reclaim Utøya. At the same time, they were advised by the authorities that the survivors and the bereaved families clearly had different needs that day. As a result, the AUF considered that the right thing to do, for several reasons, was not to have the different groups on the island at the same time. The families were therefore not allowed free access to Utøya as they themselves wished but instead were given time slots indicating when they were welcome and when they had to stay away. The morning was reserved for the families of the victims, and the AUF's own gathering would happen in the middle of the day. After a lot of discussions prior to the event, however, the plans were changed so that the families could also come to Utøya after five o'clock in the afternoon. This was important for many of them, as they felt a strong need to be on the island where their children had been killed at the precise time it happened.

Many of the bereaved were unhappy with the way the AUF had treated them. Several thought the organization came across as arrogant. The way this commemoration was planned and carried out was to have repercussions for the subsequent handling of July 22 and Utøya. The conflict surrounding the first anniversary had nothing to do with AUF survivors grieving any less than the bereaved families. It was simply a question of different needs and ways of dealing with grief and trauma. Many survivors consider the anniversary to be an important event in their own recovery process, yet time after time I have later been told how painful the AUF's decision regarding this day was for many of the bereaved.

Around the time of the first anniversary, the discussions about Utøya's future also started to come to a head. Not only did more people question whether the unanimous support the AUF had received to return to Utøya had been right, but the discourse also became more aggressive. In an opinion piece in *Aftenposten*, a major newspaper in Norway, AUF member Bjørn Ihler—himself an Utøya survivor—wrote that "Utøya should be preserved as a place for quiet contemplation.... Don't trample on the graves. Don't open up the scars from this national trauma." Several of the bereaved families agreed: "Utøya should be a place of remembrance and the AUF should find themselves somewhere else to have their summer camp." Tore Sinding Bekkedal, another AUF member and Utøya survivor, responded to this in an opinion piece saying: "If we give up the island now, the place will mostly be remembered for how it was destroyed. If we keep it, it will symbolize the fact that when fascism raised its ugly head once more, our generation didn't budge an inch."

On August 24, the perpetrator received his sentence. Judge Wenche Elizabeth Arntzen (granddaughter of Sven Arntzen, the director of public prosecutions who convicted the Nazis after the Second World War) left no room for doubt in the verdict she delivered. Breivik was declared criminally sane and sentenced to the maximum term in prison. "At the time of his release, the democracy that the defendant wants to abolish will still exist. Norway will still have inhabitants of different ethnic backgrounds, different cultures and different religions." Arntzen stressed that the terrorist had failed in his future goals as well. The society he had attacked would live on.

News, information, and important events regarding July 22 and Utøya came in rapid succession that summer. At the beginning of September the AUF presented its plans for Utøya.

After I left Norway to start studying in England, the AUF had worked intensively within the organization itself. One of the most important things it had done was to hire the small Oslo-based design firm Fantastic Norway. As their way of helping Utøya, the architects had offered to organize a public involvement process and feasibility study to consider the implications of redeveloping the island. Work began on finding a solution for what the AUF themselves wanted Utøya to be—and not to be.

During a press conference held at Youngstorget, Eskil Pedersen and Martin Henriksen presented the results of this project. In front of the entire press corps, they said that the new Utøya would reflect engagement and participation but also that a memorial would be raised on the island.

Martin said that the guiding principle behind the project had been that Utøya was primarily a place for the younger generation. What was wanted were new buildings, a new beach, and an upgraded Path of Love. "We will preserve the spirit of Utøya as we now try to move on. We will take all the good things with us," he said. Something that would not be preserved, however, was the Cafeteria building. It was here that thirteen young people had been killed, and it was here that the physical traces of the terror attacks were most evident. It would also be possible to demolish the Pump House, where fourteen young people had been executed, if so desired. The Cafeteria would be replaced by a new building. Demolition work could start that very autumn, and the new Utøya could be ready in 2014.

I followed the press conference closely. After all, this was what I had worked so hard to prepare for in the months following the terror attacks. I sent Martin a message congratulating him on the plans. Not long afterward my phone pinged. "What are you going to do when you get back to Norway? Do you want a job?"

Nine months after moving to England I was back at Youngstorget, now as CEO of Utøya. I had my master's degree, and I had left academia behind. I could choose if I wanted to share an office with the Norwegian Confederation of Trade Unions or the AUF. I chose the AUF, on the eighth floor of the People's Theater building, as close as possible to the people I was going to work with and for. And while the boards covering the windows had gone, the doors at the entrance were now upgraded with bullet-proof glass.

A small island of huge importance

I am now very familiar with the bends in the road up and down Solli-høgda. It takes thirty minutes to drive from my house to the quay where our ferry, MS *Thorbjørn*, waits to take me over to Utøya. I always have a mug of freshly brewed coffee with me in the car, and I have had a lot of interesting phone calls during the commute. The autumn weather can be quite different on each side of this 340 meter high hill between Bærum and Hole. It's often sunny with barely a cloud in the sky when I set off from Bærum, where I live. The green woods slowly but surely change color on the way. The forest turns yellow then orange then red as the autumn leaves its mark.

As I pass the pedestrian bridge at the top, I drive into a thick fog. For many years I felt that there was something symbolic about this fog, which was often dense and difficult to maneuver in, heavy and gray. Inspiration and joy were often replaced by sadness and a lack of optimism. But the fog doesn't stay there forever; it clears up after a while. That was what happened with our process in recent years, and that is what happens today. Slowly but surely rays of sun appear through the fog, and the beautiful hills around the Tyrifjord lake light up.

I leave the motorway and continue down to Utstranda, passing houses and cottages along the water's edge before I arrive. My mug is empty now. Two cups of extrastrong coffee has given me a good start to the day. As usual, I am five minutes late and as usual, Jon greets me with a smile and a laugh. He has already been at work for some time. We cast off, and MS *Thorbjørn* backs slowly out into the cold waters of the Tyrifjord. For Jon, Utøya's skipper and maintenance manager, the days have started this way for thirty years. For me it's almost ten years now. Even though the staff here have a different boat we can use, which helps to ensure that events are run efficiently, everyone prefers to be fetched by Jon on board MS *Thorbjørn*. Seeing the ferry slowly glide through the still water, with the morning mist and fog covering the lake like a veil, is the best way to greet the day. The roof of the cockpit slopes slightly down from the highest point by the steering wheel toward the seats at the back of the boat. Being six foot two, I have to stand right at the front. I shall blame the screws in the roof if I soon get a bald patch as they always pull out a few hairs. It's safest to stand at the front here with Jon all the same.

A solitary swan swims nonchalantly along the water's edge. It's completely still today. Most of the boats in the area are on shore for the winter season, so we are alone with the swan this early morning. The long thin island lies parallel to the mainland. Our office—the nicest office in the whole of Norway, in my humble opinion—is in the large white building, with UTØYA written in big red letters over the door. It's a stylish old house from the 1860s, which like many other things here shows signs of ingenious DIY solutions and a long history. When trader Gunerius Pettersen bought the island in the Tyrifjord for his own private use in 1867, one of the first things he did was to build a holiday home. This was what today is known as the Main Building (Hovedhuset). In 1898 the island was sold to Jens Kristian Meinich Bratlie. Bratlie had an impressive military and political career and was both prime minister and minister of defense in Norway. In the late 1920s Bratlie joined Vidkun Quisling's circle, and it was during this period that he used Utøya as his personal summer residence. In 1932 Utøya was taken over by the labor movement. It is somewhat surprising that at a time of severe conflict between the political right and left, Bratlie chose to sell Utøya to the arch enemy.

It's just me and Jon here today. We usually begin Mondays by planning the activities and projects for the week, but there isn't much going on at the moment, so we have another cup of coffee. Our desks are in the room most AUF members know as the reception area. The Main Building is the center of operations when the AUF holds its summer camp here. If you have any questions for those in charge, this is where to go. Information is spread from here to the camp participants, either via notice boards hanging in the Storehouse or via the old sound system. Much to the neighbors' relief, we have now dropped the loudspeakers that were dotted around the whole island. Now we just use an app.

The pink 1860s walls light up the room. A bust of Lenin stands on the shelf, with a stuffed owl on his left. Vladimir and the owl have been here for years. On the walls there are photos from the old days. Jens, Gro, a young Reiulf Steen. All former leaders of the Labor Party. Monica Bøsei— "Mother Utøya." On the table there's a couple of files, a brochure about wastewater treatment plants, a small pile of bills, some gaffer tape, and the latest copy of the *New York Times* featuring an article about Utøya. Our coffee is ready, and we enter the light blue meeting room. The sun has broken through the fog now. The conservatory with its comfy chairs is the perfect place for a chat over coffee. This is the southernmost room in the building, with yellow walls, green plants, and an ancient typewriter on an almost as ancient desk.

Of the many thousands of visitors to Utøya in recent decades, not very many have actually been in here, inside the most iconic building on the island. It has housed Prime Minister Bratlie, generations of AUF leaders have organized their summer camps from here, and last but not least, it has been the office and home of Jon and Monica, who ran Utøya together for many, many years.

At the same time as we wanted to preserve the Utøya vibe contained in these rooms, it was necessary to upgrade the building in order to use it as a center for all our activities. There was a fascinating mixture of interiors and at times a bizarre use of rooms. The conservatory was used as a laundry. The building simply had to be renovated in keeping with a new era and new functions. The before and after pictures wouldn't look out of place in an interior design magazine. The colors of the rooms are typical of the period when the house was built. Pink in the office, pale blue timber walls in the meeting room. Up the stairway the wall is pale green, adorned with camp posters from the 1950s, '60s, and '70s.

I have finished my coffee, and there's work to be done. I leave our office in the Main Building and go out into the yard. It's a traditional old yard, with the red Barn, raised red Storehouse, and white Main Building. The road divides in two, going down to the jetty in one direction and up to the top of the island in the other. Here, a few meters from the west side of the Barn, is the hillside (*Bakken*), the political heart of Utøya. Midway between the water and the highest point on the island we find this "natural" amphitheater. At the bottom of the hillside there's a simple little stage, right next to the Barn ramp. This is where inspirational talks and debates have shaped Utøya over the decades. Prime ministers, party leaders, and high-profile politicians have expressed their visions, opinions, and initiatives. Political winds have blown from Utøya across the whole of Norway, and political winds have also blown back in. In 2010 Jens Stoltenberg described Utøya as "one of the most influential places in Norwegian politics, and one of the places that has influenced Norwegian politics the most in recent years. In the summer, Utøya is Norway's most important political platform."

The yard is lit by old light fixtures that eager friends of Utøya have brought with them over the years. Gifts such as these and the efforts of volunteers have left their mark on this island, and history has certainly done so too. At the top of the roof of the Main Building there's a large sun cross—an equilateral cross inside a circle. The sun cross is known to be an ancient magical or religious symbol; it is also used for decoration in almost all the great cultures around the world and is one of the most widespread graphic depictions found in Norway. In 1933 the sun cross became the official emblem of Vidkun Quisling's national socialist fascist party, Nasjonal Samling or NS (meaning National Union). From 1942 it was used as Norway's official symbol, replacing the national coat of arms on stamps used by government agencies.

The symbol probably dates from when the Main Building was built in the 1860s, but during the Second World War—and the German occupation of Norway—it went from having a decorative function to something more significant. In the summer of 1941 much of Norwegian society was Nazified, including the trade union movement. Regime-friendly leaders took charge of the Norwegian Confederation of Trade Unions and local organizations in the trade union movement, and NS-run holiday camps were arranged on Utøya. The NS party flag, a yellow sun cross on a red background, was flown from the flagpole on Utøya that summer. Hundreds of children came here during the course of the war.

Toward the end of the war in March 1945, Utøya was taken over by Milorg, the military wing of the Norwegian resistance. When the Milorg units were warned of an imminent German raid, they evacuated their cells, and one of them sought refuge on Utøya. Loaded down with weapons, food, and equipment, they made their way across the ice on the Tyrifjord and settled in the building at the top of the island known as "Feriekolonien." When the danger was over and the group could return across the ice to the mainland, they took everything with them. The sun cross at the top of the Main Building was left untouched by the resistance fighters, however, and it hangs there to this day.

The Barn (Arbeidsmiljølåven), which dates from the 1600s, is an important part of this yard. It has been in a poor condition in recent years. It was used as a warehouse for the AUF from the 1950s, and after a while it also provided sleeping quarters. We soon decided that this couldn't continue, mainly because of the fire risk. So what could we do with this building? We have been mindful of achieving a good balance between the different aspects of history here on Utøya. The dark side must not be allowed to overshadow the light. Utøya has always been a place for political engagement, solidarity, debate, active participation, and the free exchange of views. In other words, democracy in practice. This is precisely why the terrorist came to Utøya: to destroy its democratic powerhouse.

In order to understand why Utøya was singled out for a right-wing extremist terror attack and why Utøya has acquired such an important position in Norwegian political history, it's also important for new generations to get to know the major events of the island's history. Finding a place and a way to present this background therefore became a central focus of our work. The Barn was to house an exhibition.

The building was seriously damaged by damp and rot. There were holes in the roof, a lot of bad paneling, and the ramp was rotten. We started work on restoring the Barn in the spring of 2018. The roof and the paneling were replaced. It was gradually transformed into an exhibition hall displaying the island's long history, including the period after July 22.

I pick up a broom and sweep some leaves off the stage. There's a thin layer of frost on the ground, and the planks in the small ramp are slippery. I hold onto the handrail as I get out my keys; then I open the door and go in. The ramp leads us into the Barn and back in time.

While owned by the labor movement, the island was used as a holiday camp for working-class children and teenagers in the 1930s. Utøya soon became a very popular summer destination and was used by a number of the movement's organizations, offering courses in politics, public health, and recreational sports.

The AUF's first training course on Utøya took place in the summer of 1937. Young people from all over the country were given in-depth political instruction. The Labor Party had come to power two years earlier and was implementing comprehensive social reforms. The ongoing civil war in Spain was also a major part of the program, as well as a recurrent topic of conversation around the campfires at night.

A new chapter of the island's history began in 1950, when the Oslo and Akershus Trade Union Confederation gave Utøya to the AUF as a fiftieth anniversary present. The moment the AUF took over, a massive program of volunteer work began—a tradition that has become part of Utøya's identity.

Utøya has since been used as a "political laboratory" for the AUF's mother party on many occasions, whether the Labor Party has been in government or opposition. Labor politicians have, for example, used Utøya and AUF members as a kind of "listening post" in their efforts to improve Norwegian schools. Ever since the AUF started prioritizing environmental issues in the early 1990s, they have regularly criticized the party leadership for having low ambitions in their climate and environment policies. When it comes to foreign policy, the demand from Utøya has been for Norway to promote peace efforts more actively, both during the Spanish Civil War in the 1930s and later during the Vietnam War and in Iraq and Afghanistan. A more liberal approach to asylum and refugees has also been important to AUF members on Utøya, and many ministers of justice have struggled to justify Norway's restrictive immigration policies to them.

I go further into the Barn. With each step you take, you learn more about this little island's history. In addition to all the unfamiliar faces on the walls, there are also many photos from Utøya of people we recognize from Norwegian history books. Party secretary Haakon Lie, exiled revolutionary Leon Trotsky, justice minister and the first secretary general of the UN Trygve Lie, prime minister Einar Gerhardsen, party leader Reiulf Steen, state secretary (and later convicted spy) Arne Treholt, AUF leader Thorbjørn Jagland, foreign minister Thorvald Stoltenberg, prime minister Gro Harlem Brundtland, and many others.

In the middle of the end wall of the Barn we have put in a large window, providing a panoramic view of the soccer pitch. The soccer tournament held during the AUF camp can undoubtedly be considered a major highlight. Over the years, players have impressed everyone with their physical prowess, command of the ball, determination, and prestigious victories. Soccer and politics have gone hand in hand, and matches have often been an important way of achieving reconciliation after tough political infighting.

The operational aspect of Utøya's history is full of ups and downs. When the Labor Party was still in power in the early 1960s, there was growth and progress in Norway, and the AUF maintained a high level of activity, not least on Utøya. The decade began with one of the biggest camps ever: over fifteen hundred young people from the whole of Scandinavia descended on the island. These years were full of optimism, with almost seven thousand visitors each season. However, from the mid-1960s the interest in Utøya waned. While the AUF had all the reason in the world to be proud of its wonderful property in the Tyrifjord, there was no disguising the fact that running costs posed a huge challenge for the organization. A memo about Utøya addressed to the AUF executive board meeting on December 10, 1965, concluded: "It is proposed that the island be sold." The AUF's finances were seriously affected by the economic burden Utøya represented, and selling the island seemed to be the only solution. Something hindering this, however, was the stipulation in the deed of gift from 1950 that the trade union movement had to approve the sale in advance, which it didn't. Discussions about selling the island continued in the following years without any of the attempts succeeding. In the meantime, the national committee decided that the island should be completely shut down. In secret, and despite a ban on using the island, there was a small group from Oslo that continued to go to Utøya all the same. Their stubbornness and perseverance finally paid off when in April 1969 they won approval to open up the island again. Utøya would remain in the AUF's hands after all.

There was further uncertainty and reorganization in 1990. The AUF decided that the organization should mainly concentrate on politics, while others should be in charge of matters that were not the AUF's prime concern. This also had consequences for Utøya. The limited company that was set up was given responsibility for running the island and its finances, as well as a mandate to turn Utøya into something more than just the AUF's own campground.

This was the start of a new era for Utøya, even though the economic situation was still precarious. The company went bankrupt but got back on its feet again. Until 2011 the profit margins and turnover were low. The island entirely depended on annual support from the AUF and other members of the labor movement. It's easy to see how the tough economic conditions affected Utøya, considering the island's cheap but clever solutions, creative use of buildings, and simple standards.

I leave the Barn, and turning southward I am met by a gentle wind. The big birch between the Main Building and the volleyball court rustles its beautiful yellow leaves. I give the tree an appreciative nod. I have wandered past this tree so many times. This is where I hang my hammock in the summer. This tree has seen so much—from the best life has to offer to the very worst.

The road goes past the birch tree, continuing south from the Main Building to the Schoolhouse (Skolestua). I walk down to the garage. There's also a sauna here, or what the biography of the island describes as "an old hot dog stand taken from Youngstorget, insulated with 22 years' worth of *Arbeiderbladet*" (the newspaper previously owned by the Labor Party). "The stove was found on a rubbish heap in Hole. So were the bricks. The only investment had been some mortar. When it was lit, flames came out of the chimney." The sauna is still here. For several years it was an important institution on Utøya, but it hasn't been used for a while now.

South of the sauna is the Bay of Pigs (Grisebukta), or Menshevik Cove, as it used to be known. There are lots of references to communism and the Soviet Union on Utøya. One of the highlights of the island's history was when a world-famous revolutionary came to visit in 1936. Leon Trotsky was, together with Lenin, one of the two main leaders of the Bolshevik Revolution in 1917. Trotsky built up the Soviet Red Army, and he was first commissar for foreign affairs and then war commissar in the Bolshevik government. Lenin's death in 1924 led to a power struggle among the communist leaders—a struggle in which Trotsky finally lost out to Stalin.

Trotsky was thrown out of the government and lost all his influential positions in the communist party one after the other. In 1929 he was accused of being a traitor and exiled from the Soviet Union. He first fled to Turkey, then France, and finally Norway in June 1935, where he was granted temporary asylum. In the summer of 1936 Trotsky visited Utøya frequently. Here he worked on one of his most important book projects, his wide-ranging critique of Joseph Stalin. It's not unlikely that the last details of his legendary book *The Revolution Betrayed* were actually written in the Main Building on Utøya.

During the late summer and autumn the situation came to a head. The government was put under massive pressure by the Russians, and both Conservatives and National Socialists in Norway demanded his deportation. Trotsky said the Norwegian government was kowtowing to the fascists by wanting him out of the country. "In just a few years you yourselves will be the victims of fascism!" he warned prophetically.

On December 7, 1936, the government decided not to renew Trotsky's residence permit in Norway, and the Mexican government agreed to give him refuge. Late in the evening of December 19, Trotsky went on board a tanker and left Norway for good. He lived in Mexico until he was assassinated by a Soviet agent on August 20, 1940.

I continue along the road. With the Bay of Pigs below me, I enter a mass of green trees. Just here and there an autumn-colored aspen or rowan blazes orange amid all the greenery. After about a hundred meters it opens up. The deciduous forest is golden. The sun is low in the sky. All its rays are concentrated on the southern part of the island, with the sunbeams fighting their way through the leaves to light up the four red buildings in the woods. The largest of these, the Schoolhouse, has stood here for some time.

The Schoolhouse was built in the 1950s from materials that the Germans had used for roadworks along Utstranda during the war. Norway's first female prime minister Gro Harlem Brundtland has told the tale of how she learned to force open doors here when she was little. She was with her parents at the camp, and when the evening came, she and the other children had to go to bed. The Schoolhouse provided accommodation for families at the time, and the young Gro didn't think it was fair that the adults could have all the really interesting discussions without the children around. With some tools they found in the bedroom, the children forced open the door, sneaked out, and hid in the bushes around the campfire, where they secretly listened to the adults' conversations.

It hasn't been usual for AUF members to bring their own children to camp for a long time, so the Schoolhouse has in recent years offered relatively basic, yet exclusive, sleeping accommodation. If you suffer from allergies, you can ask to sleep indoors during your stay at the camp. This

No Man Is an Island 23

is probably where you would be given a bed, in a dormitory with up to five others.

There's a lot of dense vegetation growing around the Schoolhouse. Much too dense. In the old days there was a handball court on the grass here, but now it's overgrown with birch and aspen trees, thorn bushes and bracken. We have quite a job to do here, I think to myself as I make my way through the trees to the back of the building. The tall pine trees lose all their needles at this time of year, and the gutters are full of them.

I fetch the ladder lying by the north wall of the building and carefully climb up it. As I thought, the gutter is blocked. Even though I am in my normal clothes, I can just as well do some maintenance work now that I am up here. I scoop out handful after handful of twigs, pine needles, and withered leaves. Water splashes over the edge, running down my trouser legs and the red planks of the façade. The blockage in the gutter has gone and the water can flow normally again.

From the ladder I have a view of Thranesletta. This area was once named after the leader of the first political mass movement organized in Norway, Marcus Thrane. Once the first association of working men was founded in 1848, the Thrane movement soon became a major political force in the fight to improve conditions for Norwegian workers. However, just as the movement gradually disappeared, his name has also gone out of use on Utøya.

On my way down the ladder, I peer in through the window. Inside is a little sitting room with a fireplace, two groups of sofas and armchairs, and a bookcase in the corner. There are historical pictures hanging on the gray walls. A couple of board games are still out on one of the tables. The rooms have a different feel than they had before. Until 2013 they reflected interior decorating trends from both the past and the present: red walls, pink sofas, and white IKEA lamps.

On July 22 it wasn't possible to look in through the windows: they were barricaded with mattresses and furniture.

A mixture of luck and extreme bravery meant that the forty-seven people who had sought refuge here during the shooting actually survived. They hid in the sitting room, bedrooms, and showers. Many of those who survived July 22 by taking refuge in the Schoolhouse helped to do up the building in the years that followed, painting the walls and assembling new furniture. This was a simple but important way of bringing the building back to normality and processing traumas at the same time.

I get down from the ladder and walk around to the front of the building. At the other end of the yard there's a little row of outhouses. The outhouses on Utøya contain the toilets that are probably the ones most frequently cleaned by future and present prime ministers in Norway. The buildings on Utøya have always had a basic standard. To appreciate the charm of some of these it helps to already be in love with the island. Outside toilets are certainly charming, but given the choice, the youth of today would no doubt prefer luxury to nostalgia.

Where the road turns northward and back up to the campground, a small detour winds its way through the woods, out to the water: this legendary path on Utøya is known as "Kjærlighetsstien," or the Path of Love. The path goes the whole way along the south, west, and north coast of the island, from Nakenodden (Naked Point) in the south to Bolsjevika (Bolshevik Cove) in the north. The sounds change as you leave the road, which is surrounded by dense woods on all sides, and head out on the path on the southwest of the island. The wind blows through the trees, and it's the trees you hear rather than the wind itself. With every step I take toward the path and the edge of the island, I become more aware of the wind. The sound of wind, water, and waves creates a completely different atmosphere on the path than in the interior of the island.

A stroll along the Path of Love evokes Utøya's two-fold legacy like nowhere else. Going for a walk here is one of the nicest things you can do on the island, but also one of the most painful. I have heard a lot of moving stories from this path, even after July 22, 2011. I am sure that romance and love have flourished here in recent years too, but I am also quite sure that nothing beats my favorite story from 1958. An elderly couple told it to me during a visit to Utøya a few years ago.

Two teenagers went to Utøya to take part in the AUF camp at Whitsun that year. They were going to spend a whole week on the island. For several days they flirted, got to know each other, and soon fell head over heels in love. The boy and the girl came from different parts of the country, and they knew it would be hard to stay in touch. The girl wasn't very keen to tell her parents that she had fallen in love with a boy at a political camp on Utøya either. "Flirting like that is simply not proper," she could imagine her mother saying. When the camp was about to end, the boy therefore decided to raise the stakes. He broke into the kitchen of the Cafeteria and stole a can. Later in the day, as the sun was setting over the Tyrifjord, he invited his beloved for an evening stroll along the Path of Love. Against a backdrop of the red setting sun, and while the other AUF members were discussing Mao's Great Leap Forward and the creation of the European Economic Community the two of them were alone on the path. On the western tip of the island, high above the water, with a wonderful view of the lake and the most beautiful sunset in the history of the world (according to them, at least), the boy went down on one knee and took out the can. "Will you marry me?" he asked, holding out a ring of pineapple. "Yes!" exclaimed the girl without a moment's hesitation, and the boy slipped the dripping pineapple ring on her outstretched finger.

They were thrilled to tell me this tale almost sixty years later, still hand in hand and happily married. Aurora, my now nine-year-old daughter, often asks me to tell her the "pineapple story" at bedtime. If Aurora or anyone else would like to recreate the proposal sometime in the future, we shall certainly make sure there's a couple of cans of pineapple on the shelf in the storeroom.

The topography of the west coast of Utøya is different from where the ferry docks. The cliffs and precipices make for a dramatic but beautiful walk around the edge of the island, high above the water. The blanket of spruces and pines covering Utøya comes to an abrupt end where the cliffs plunge down to the water. This is heaven on earth, love and pineapple. A few meters further on, it's hell.

There are roses attached to the fence. A plaque inscribed with the name Åsta Sofie hangs around the tree by the path. She and ten others were shot on the Path of Love. Only one survived. On the steep slope below, five young people were killed and several more seriously injured. Many hid in the caves and cliffs right under the path.

I have walked along the Path of Love countless times these past years. At the bend, with the slope down to the water on my left and the woods on my right, with the path teetering on the edge of the cliffs in front of me, the stories from the darkest day always come back to me.

The roses are left by bereaved families when they visit the island at different times of the year. They hang there on the fence until they wither and have to be thrown away. I pull at a dead rose. It's securely attached and difficult to remove. The dark red petals fall to the ground, and just the stalk remains. I work it free and take off the leaves. Part of our job is to get rid of flowers, letters, and other things that people leave here, so that the area always looks nice and dignified.

From this part of Utøya you can see across the Tyrifjord. It's a couple of kilometers to the mainland west of Utøya from here. You are high up, and the wind is often quite strong. It's often completely quiet all the same. The wind envelops you, shuts you off from the rest of island life, silencing everything around you. We don't often have the time or space for serious reflection in our daily lives. The world's secrets are hidden inside silence, writes explorer and author Erling Kagge in his book about silence. Silence is a luxury and a tool that we should appreciate and make use of as much as we can. Shutting the world out is not a question of turning our backs on our surroundings, which is often necessary in our hectic and noisy existence, but rather something we can do in order to see things more clearly. This is such a place. Silence and reflection.

The Path of Love continues northward. I enter the area called the Buskerud camp. From this small plateau I leave the path and walk toward the campground. The first thing I see here is the green, T-shaped shower block, obviously designed to be practical and inexpensive rather than attractive. Situated in the corner of the campground, it provides toilets, showers, and some basic living accommodation.

The expanse of grass spreads outward, slanting down in a southerly direction. It is encircled by golden pine trunks, and at the other end of the campground is an outdoor stage. This is new, built by Swedish apprentices in the spring of 2016. There was a similar stage here earlier, the source of many unforgettable experiences for thousands of young AUF members. Music has always been an important part of the events arranged on Utøya.

The biggest tree in the campground is known as the Value Tree. Visitors have hung value notes from the branches of this old pine tree in recent years, notes containing words or messages about something that is important to them: "International solidarity," "Utøya," "Peace on earth," "Mum and Dad," "We will never forget you." A lot of these notes have appeared spontaneously, written by people attending some kind of event. Others have been hung there as part of the course the writer has taken part in. Jotting down a few simple words is a good way to get thought processes started. It can be an important element in an educational program, which is why we actively encourage it. The value notes hanging from the branches flutter in the wind, shining like jewelry. The tree and the values we believe in light up when darkness falls.

This large area of grass is the essence of Utøya, in a practical, symbolic, and historical sense—right up to present day. Here at the campground you can feel the pulse of the summer camp rise and fall. It is often said that the headquarters of the labor movement aren't at Youngstorget in Oslo—that's just for the party bosses. Since the labor movement took over the island, it is Utøya that has been the heart of the AUF and the movement. For generations, the island has been a unique arena for left-wing youth wishing to combine political activism with leisure time.

In the mid-1970s, Thorbjørn Jagland, Jens Stoltenberg, and many other important figures in the history of the Labor Party and of Norway would sit around the campfire on Utøya listening to party veterans like Einar Gerhardsen and Trygve Bratteli talk about politics and the past. They told the teenagers about seeing Lenin at meetings in Moscow, battles during the Spanish Civil War, and what it was like to be in a German prison camp during World War II. Political instruction and spreading awareness have been the focus of numerous courses, meetings, gatherings, and not least the traditional Whitsun and summer camps, which attract up to a thousand young people from all over the country, plus international guests.

At the same time, the island has been much more than just politics. Although many thousands of teenagers have spent hot summer days here over the years, only a few have become full-time politicians. Very many still associate their stay on Utøya with carefree holidays, sun, swimming, and summer. "It nearly always rains at the summer camps on Utøya but when I think back, I only remember sunshine all the same," they say.

It's most common to hear such romanticized reminiscences about the Utøya camps from the island's veterans. The weather gets better and better the longer ago you were there. People talk of the Utøya feeling, the special sensation the camps gave the participants—the feeling of being on an isolated island for an entire week, where you can be yourself among people who share your values and visions for society, the feeling of solidarity, fellowship, and involvement.

The campfire every evening has become an institution. The tales told by the older and more experienced members are a great inspiration for the new participants at the camp. Everyone sings old working-class songs. When night falls not everyone chooses to go to bed, though. A lot of them reckon that sleep can wait until they get home.

To get people up in the morning, out of their tents, along to breakfast, and over to the political workshops, loud music is blasted, preferably the latest in techno. Towels, swimwear, soggy T-shirts, and dirty trousers are hung out to dry from the guy ropes of the tents. International guests lend an exotic feel to the proceedings, and political rallying calls adorn banners and flags. The campground is a jumble of colors and chaos, in a happy mix of old traditions and contemporary camping life.

The highlight of the summer— and hell on earth

The campground and all the activity it symbolizes were the main focus of the increasingly fraught discussions that took place toward the end of 2012. Political engagement, idealism, friendship, tolerance, and holidays. The Utøya feeling. This island had shaped the lives of thousands of people and given them their most cherished memories. But Utøya no longer simply stood for these positive things. Now it was associated with terror, grief, and loss.

When I returned from England after my studies and started to work with Utøya again that autumn, I soon realized that the first plans for the island exposed the huge disparity between impatient, forward-looking AUF members and many of the bereaved and others who were struggling with grief after the terrorist attack.

The events of July 22 naturally led to a broader ownership of Utøya. Far more people rightly felt a connection to the place, and consequently there were more groups with strong feelings about what the island should stand for in the future: the bereaved, those who survived the attack, active AUF members who weren't there when the shooting took place but were the ones who would use Utøya again. There were the Utøya veterans and future generations of youngsters who hadn't yet been to the island—they could all relate to Utøya and they all had an opinion.

On October 27, 2012, I attended my first meeting of the county leaders of the national July 22 support group.

The national support group after July 22 was founded in Oslo on August 21, 2011, to promote the interests of all those concerned. The support group is open to anyone affected: those who were in or near the government quarter or at the AUF summer camp on Utøya, their families and closest contacts, and those who in other ways were involved or affected by the attacks. It was still the parents of the victims that made up the majority of those present at the meeting at Gardermoen.

Even though the presentation for the support group contained many of the "right" phrases—"there will be a memorial on Utøya," "we will have a close dialogue with the bereaved," "our goal is not to do this as fast as possible but to do it properly"—the visual illustrations were full of youngsters enjoying themselves in the lake, concerts, optimism, and enthusiasm. A new beach was planned for the Bay of Pigs, for example.

Some people were left with the impression that the AUF was going to turn Utøya into a water park. It's entirely understandable that many found the plans unacceptable. They had the feeling that swimming and fun had trumped gravity and grief. There was little evidence of a willingness to deal with the traumatic, painful sides of Utøya's recent history.

Nothing made this plainer than the decision to demolish the Cafeteria, the building where thirteen young people were killed and the only place that had visible physical traces of the shooting. The Pump House, where fourteen were killed right outside, could also be torn down if the bereaved so wished.

The meeting room buzzed with feelings, insults, and accusations. Several of those affected said that it was too early for the AUF to consider arranging a summer camp on Utøya again, at least for the time being. It was also obvious to me how well rooted the plans for the island were in the AUF's own organization, but how little it took into consideration almost all the others concerned.

During this period we also received a letter signed by many of the affected families. The letter made it clear that a large number of them did not support the plans to rebuild Utøya and thought that the island should be designated as a conservation area. Precisely this word "conservation" was to dominate the debate about Utøya for years to come, even though it meant very different things to different people. The letter sent in September 2012 was seen by many as arguing against the Utøya plans, against activity, life, and engagement. In this way it was also the direct opposite of what the AUF wanted. The wish for conservation was interpreted as an argument for making Utøya into purely a commemorative site, where time stands frozen at the moment terror struck, and thus a memorial landscape in the spirit of Auschwitz, for example. However, the entire content of the letter we received, signed by a number of the bereaved and other affected people, was considerably more complex and wide-ranging than most people understood it to be. The actual content was to become an important issue in the subsequent conversations we had with the people behind the letter. As was the case in very many of the other ensuing discussions, it was the details that were telling, not the headlines.

As a way of following up the letter, a group of the bereaved asked the Directorate for Cultural Heritage to place a conservation order on Utøya. The directorate quickly decided, however, that Utøya and its buildings were not covered by the relevant provisions for conservation matters. The letter and the reply from the directorate received a lot of attention in the media, and the debate about Utøya's future soon became public and heated.

There was quite obviously an abyss between those who remembered the long, meaningful, positive history of the island on the one hand and those who only remembered what happened that terrible, meaningless, dark Friday in July on the other. And of course there were also many whose best and worst memories were of Utøya, and they were caught in between.

It wasn't hard to understand that those who were directly affected by the terrorist attack, and the bereaved in particular, could feel this way. First, not so much time had passed since it happened. In the course of that first year, there had been massive coverage of the incident, the trial, hate ideology, emergency preparedness, the victims, and the bereaved. The grieving process was very delayed for some people, and when the trial and first anniversary commemoration ceremonies were finally over, the plans for Utøya felt like a slap in the face. Second, Utøya had almost become sacred ground for some of those affected. For many, reopening the island would mean undermining the powerful symbol of Utøya as a place of execution for sixty-nine innocent people.

The emotions sparked by the plans to rebuild the island were intensified by polished images of teenagers at play. The whole thing also felt too rushed. Very many of those most directly involved hadn't yet been included in the processes regarding the future of Utøya. Moreover, the way the AUF had treated the bereaved in connection with the first anniversary commemoration—when there hadn't been a proper dialogue and the families had been excluded from important decisions—had left deep and painful scars.

On the other hand, there were both AUF members and bereaved families who wanted Utøya to be rebuilt. They wanted the place back, as a kind of victory over and protest against the perpetrator and his objective. In fact, most of those affected generally took this view. Utøya is the heart of the AUF, and since 1950 thousands of youngsters have made new friends, received political instruction, and undergone personal development there. Reclaiming Utøya and resuming almost normal activity as soon as possible was seen as a way for the AUF to make a comeback after the attack; people thought it would be a healing process for the organization. The idea that everything would go back to normal, that the AUF could return to the paradise that Utøya had once been, was a source of huge comfort to many AUF survivors at a time when nothing was as before.

In the following weeks, the national support group sent out questionnaires to all the counties asking what members thought about Utøya's future. A great many wanted Utøya to live on. It was especially important to a lot of them that the AUF's summer camp should return. It was crystal clear, however, that all county branches wanted more time to consider the question of demolition, more time for plans to be developed, and more time before activities were resumed on the island.

As a result of this action undertaken internally by the support group's county branches, the national board sent a letter to the AUF in December 2012. The letter recommended a period of reflection until the end of 2014, postponing major building works in the meantime, and it stressed the importance of better dialogue going forward.

There was enormous pressure on the AUF and those of us working with Utøya that autumn. The media, affected families, and five million Norwegians all had something to say. A lot of the strongest opinions were often completely contradictory. The controversy was dominated by feelings, speculation, and self-appointed experts. In the opinion columns of newspapers around the country there were headlines such as "Are we dancing on their graves?" and "This is our Auschwitz."

No Man Is an Island 33

This is where we stood. Having given a forward-looking presentation with solutions and a clear direction, we were now stuck in an emotionally demanding, chaotic deadlock. We had no previous experience of this kind of work. We received no offers of help from the public authorities. People who had personally suffered a brutal terrorist attack were responsible for handling the process completely alone.

What should we do now?

Hate must never win

AUF leader Eskil Pedersen had declared, "We will reclaim Utøya" as early as July 23, 2011. Terrorist acts must never silence politically active youth. Working for a fairer world became more important than ever before. Violence cannot dictate how we use the freedom of speech, or result in a more closed, intolerant society. To put it simply, terror must not be allowed to triumph. This basic tenet is something those of us working with Utøya since July 22, 2011, have stuck to. It has been an absolute principle.

Many people, myself included, wondered whether this actually was right. It wasn't easy to understand why the AUF was willing to undergo the painful process of reclaiming Utøya. But the whole time the answer was yes, it is necessary and it is right—for the AUF as an organization, for the labor movement, for individuals, and for Norwegian society.

The terrorist attacks of July 22 demonstrated that democracy, the freedom of expression, and an open, diverse society are also vulnerable in Norway. One of the lessons to be drawn is that we need *more* places where we can get together—not fewer. If our system is to survive, new generations must understand democracy in practice, take part in political debates, and learn to live together with differences and disagreements. This is not something you find out about from the echo chambers on the internet but by meeting other people and spending time in their company, such as teenagers have done on Utøya for seventy years. Keeping Utøya as a democratic meeting and learning arena is thus also a question of ensuring the sustainability of society.

Neither is it possible nor desirable to close down all the places that can trigger painful memories. Ground Zero isn't a conservation area, nor is the center of Oklahoma City or the train station in Madrid. Life goes on in London, Dar es Salaam, Beirut, Boston, and Bologna. When traumatic incidents occur in the heart of a community, it's always a matter of balancing the need to remember and commemorate with the need for new life. This has been achieved in Madrid, London, and Bali, plus countless other places. Some have succeeded better than others, but taking this balance into account is something we are forced to do in situations like these.

We soon realized that this balance had not been achieved, that these dilemmas and questions had not been sufficiently addressed in the first plans for Utøya. The answer to the question of what we should do now was thus simple and difficult at the same time: we had to change the plans.

We had an overall objective but lacked any direction.

Two formidable tasks

The AUF had a heavy burden to bear. It owned and was supposed to manage a historically significant island, its own movement's most valued location and scene of Norway's worst ever act of terrorism. At the same time, the AUF organization had been targeted by terror itself. Hundreds of its members had experienced deeply traumatic events, hundreds of young people had lost many of their closest friends, and a number were seriously damaged both physically and psychologically. The challenge they now faced was how to rebuild Utøya and the AUF. Both tasks were equally demanding.

The decisions the AUF made during this period were crucial for what was to follow, for Utøya and the Workers' Youth League alike. Eskil Pedersen made strategically important choices when he envisaged the division of responsibilities in this regard. The AUF naturally had to focus on its own organization to a greater extent—concentrate not only on how to build it up again but also how to prepare itself and their members to be able to arrange their traditional and important summer camps on Utøya. In practice, the reopening of Utøya was therefore left to Utøya itself. The board of Utøya was to be responsible for the process and the practical work. I became project manager and subsequently CEO.

Although the executive board and leadership of the AUF and the board and leadership of Utøya had two different functions and mandates, there wasn't exactly a Chinese wall between them. For example, I shared an office with the AUF those first few years, and we have made a large number of decisions together—despite our different tasks, mandates, and goals.

It was natural that I devoted most of my time to the bereaved, the survivors, and the process involving how Utøya should be rebuilt. The AUF was busy with its own organization's recovery and future. However, we also knew that the AUF had to take the lead in order to ensure that there would again be activity on the island. Its process therefore greatly influenced our own work.

A crucial decision made by Eskil Pedersen and the AUF in the autumn of 2012 was to bide their time, yet this decision wasn't reached without lengthy debate. There was a widespread feeling that unless the AUF was back on the island within a year or two, it would be harder to reestablish the traditions and culture of Utøya. Many AUF members were impatient; others wanted to go back to the camp themselves. For a lot of the survivors, it was their personal way of triumphing over the terrorist and processing their own traumas. Most people in the AUF—and the majority of people in youth organizations—are only active for a couple of years. They are then either too old or they have continued in party politics, lost interest, or have chosen to no longer be involved for whatever reason. If too many years passed before the AUF's camp was resumed, many of those affected felt it wouldn't be their own generation returning to it but the next one.

It became clear in the course of this discussion that teenagers and adults have a very different concept of time. A couple of years here or there is less important to a fifty-year-old mother or father than to a fifteen-year-old.

We finally decided to follow the support group's advice in its entirety. The task of rebuilding Utøya would not start for two years. The AUF would not return until at least 2015. Essential maintenance work had to be prioritized in the meantime. Not least, there had to be better dialogue in order to find better solutions.

Sanding walls and thinking of others

From the campground there's a track leading down to the water. A couple of trees have fallen over, and one of them is partially blocking the path. The trees here are mainly big old-growth mountain pines, plus the occasional huge spruce with branches all the way down to the forest floor. I get out my phone, take a picture, and send it to Jon. "Okay, I'll bring the saw and get rid of it tomorrow," he quickly replies.

It has started raining. Not just the drizzle typical of eastern Norway, but proper rain, like we have on the west coast. The raindrops gather on my hood and trickle down my jacket. They are swallowed up by the soil underfoot. Down on the shore is the Pump House, the gray building that has one simple function. This is where Utøya gets its drinking water from. The pumps inside fetch water from the pipes far out and deep down in the Tyrifjord and pump it up to the buildings around the island. An ultraviolet water purification system ensures that it's free of bacteria and safe to drink.

I leave the path and walk down to the Pump House, over the rocks along the water's edge. They are slippery and sharp, and it's steep down here. By one of the Pump House walls lies a small heart made of stone.

This is another of the painful places on Utøya. The memory of the fourteen people murdered here will always imbue it with a powerful aura. A silence always descends on this place, too. But the world cannot stop turning here either. The silence is broken by the sound of waves and leaves fluttering in the wind.

I have a tape measure with me today. I take a couple of photos and measure the distance from the top of the rocks and down to the level where the building stands. Several of the victims' parents are getting to an age when they will soon have problems navigating such a steep drop and rugged terrain. Part of managing Utøya is deciding how to keep many such places around the island accessible to everyone, including those who have difficulty walking. That's why I have come to make sketches for new steps down to the Pump House to be built in the spring. I carefully walk over to the building.

I scratch at one of the walls and see patches of red and blue appear underneath. But these colors don't belong here; they date from July 21, 2014.

The marking of the anniversary in the years following 2011 clearly exposed the tensions between the AUF and others affected by July 22, including the support group. The first anniversary in 2012 revealed that the collaboration between the Workers' Youth League and the support group was anything but ideal.

The simple solution in the following year, July 22, 2013, was for each group to organize their own ceremony. The AUF couldn't face a repeat of the discussions and criticism that arose in 2012 and therefore allowed the support group to have its entire open day and commemoration ceremony on Utøya. The AUF itself chose to mark the day with a minute's silence, speeches, and music on the quay on the mainland.

This struck me as a clear signal that we were far from enjoying the level of collaboration and dialogue we should have had. In 2014, as another anniversary approached, the big question was how the occasion should be handled. Earlier that year, Trond Blattmann and Eskil Pedersen, leader of the support group and AUF, respectively, had agreed that everyone should join together to mark the anniversary. Relations between them had clearly improved. On the evening of July 21, we gathered at Sundvolden Hotel. The support group always meets at the hotel to mark the anniversaries on Utøya. Bereaved families and survivors come from all over the country, and for many of them it's important at this time to feel supported by others in the same situation.

On the news that evening we watched a report from Utøya where they presented what would happen here the following day. I had myself shown the public broadcaster NRK around, so I more or less knew what the journalists would say. The report ended with a series of photos from around the island. Right before it was over, however, I was shocked. Without the NRK photographer apparently reacting, we were shown a glimpse of the Pump House for a moment or two with a big heart and a peace sign tagged all over it in red, white, and blue.

Just before the anniversary each July, I always go around to all the places where the attacks took place to check there is nothing untoward. That is why I had already been by the Pump House earlier in the day. The tagging must have happened right before NRK arrived, probably done by someone who had gone ashore from their own boat. I immediately went over to see if Trond Blattman had noticed anything in the report. I showed him and Kolbein Fridtun the pictures. Kolbein actually lost his daughter by the Pump House and knows the building and area well. Moreover, he knew how it felt to attend the commemoration of the anniversary and what it meant for so many people. We agreed that this could be upsetting for the families.

I asked Ole Martin Juul Slyngstadli from the AUF to join me, and together we left for Utøya at the crack of dawn the next morning. We took Utøya's little dinghy out to the island and walked down to the Pump House. The whole building was covered in graffiti. The message of peace and love was pleasant enough, so we concluded that it was probably done by some well-meaning idiots. As the paint shop hadn't yet opened, we agreed to try and remove it with a sander. We took electrical cords and equipment with us across the island and got to work.

Ole Martin had himself been by the Pump House three years earlier. He told me about the heart-wrenching scenes that had taken place here. He was in the Cafeteria building when he first heard the sharp bangs coming from the campground. "Who the hell would do something so stupid as explode firecrackers at this moment?" he said to himself. The sounds came nearer. People were screaming and running in all directions. He had to escape. Ole Martin managed to make his way out of the building and began to run toward the woods. As he fled, he turned round and spotted his friend Ina. She had collapsed outside the Cafeteria, seriously injured.

Ole Martin ran over and tried to tend to her wounds, but she had been shot several times—in her jaw, chest, and under both arms—and was bleeding profusely. Shots continued to be fired inside the Cafeteria building. Ole Martin had to get himself and Ina to safety. He lifted her in his arms and ran barefoot down toward the water. They hid in the bracken

No Man Is an Island   41

and undergrowth near the track down by the Pump House. The Path of Love goes right above the Pump House, and the track leads there from the campground. A lot of AUF members were therefore here at some point or other in the course of the seventy-two minutes of hell on the island.

When Ole Martin reached the area above the Pump House, there was already a large group hiding there. After a long period of silence, they heard someone call out: "Is there anyone alive here? The police have come. You're safe." It was about ten past six, and Ole Martin was still lying in the bracken with a couple of others in the woods by the Pump House. Everyone was focused on keeping Ina alive. "Are you really from the police?" asked a girl as she got up and walked over to him. Just then Ole Martin heard another shot and then lots more. Screams, death. Very many must have been hit.

After a while it went quiet. The perpetrator moved on, away from where Ole Martin and the others were hidden. Fourteen young people were dead and a number of others injured. The sound of shots became fainter and fainter, and then came the roar of a helicopter.

A bit later they heard a boat coming ashore. They noticed that the driver was helping teenagers into the boat, but should they really trust him to help them? They decided they had had to. Ole Martin called out that they had someone who was wounded, and then carried Ina down over the slippery, jagged rocks to the Pump House. They had to step over dead youngsters on the way. He put Ina into the boat and ran back to help the others.

Ole Martin went from one victim to the next looking for signs of life. He and another AUF member carried another seriously injured young person on board the boat. Ole Martin himself remained on the island as there were others in need of his assistance.

So now, on the same day three years later, Ole Martin was back at the Pump House again.

Plaster flew in all directions, but the color wouldn't come off. It had seeped into all the nooks and crannies of the Leca blocks. Soon there was only gray graffiti left, but it wasn't gone completely. It was almost nine and we hadn't nearly finished. In another hour, boats full of guests would start to arrive.

Ole Martin continued using the sander while I took the boat to the mainland, sped to the nearest paint shop, bought a few tins of gray paint for concrete, and came back. The sanding hadn't been terribly effective, but the paint soon did the job.

When the first guests arrived just after ten, the paint was still wet but at least the Pump House looked "normal." Listening to Ole Martin's account while we stood there sanding the walls was extremely tough. He was determined to get rid of the graffiti so that it wouldn't cause additional pain to the families about to arrive.

It was a direct reminder of what my job was all about, and what Ole Martin was now the prime example of: trying as far as possible to meet the needs of all those affected.

WINTER

The snow lies like a duvet over the ground. It's cold, minus ten degrees Celsius, and the snow creaks underfoot. I can see my breath in the cold air as I trample through the deep snow. I am wearing a thick down jacket. It can be wet and windy where I come from in the west of Norway, but the air is never as dry and cold as this.

While I walk up the track from the Pump House back to the campground, across what the rest of the year is a large green stretch of grass, heavy clouds move in from the north. Even though it's the middle of the day, it quickly gets dark.

I sit down on a cold, frosty rock. The chilly, clear air fills my lungs as I close my eyes and remain quite still. The campground here is open and exposed but not isolated. One of the strongest indications that we have achieved the outcome we wanted for this island—this balance between serious reflection and engagement, between the past and the future—is found in the interaction between the campground and the new building now standing on the small mound opposite.

After the labor movement took over Utøya in the early 1930s, a large community building was built on the plateau in the center of the island, with children's dormitories, a dining hall, and a kitchen. Originally known as Feriekolonien (the Holiday Camp), it was later called Kafébygget (the Cafeteria building). This initially brown-stained, then green-painted, barracks-like building has been the logistical heart of Utøya ever since.

People would meet in the meeting rooms, have supper in the dining hall, buy ice creams and waffles in the kiosk, and listen to speeches in the great hall when the weather was too bad to be outside.

This was where Gro Harlem Brundtland delivered her speech on the morning of that fateful day in 2011. This was also where hundreds of campers gathered to find out what had happened in Oslo. They gathered to console each other, look after each other, charge their phones, or just seek shelter from the pouring rain.

The great hall was packed when the information meeting started. There simply wasn't room for several hundred young people to be in there at once. Even with provisional support underneath the building to prop it up, the floor noticeably sagged in the middle. The weight of many years of lively youngsters had taken its toll. From the stage, Tonje Brenna, secretary general of the AUF, and Monica Bøsei, Utøya's CEO, told everyone what they knew about the situation in Oslo. While a lot of people had already heard the news before the meeting, others hadn't. Afterward, many remained inside the Cafeteria building.

When the terrorist arrived at Utøya soon after five o'clock that afternoon, he was met by Monica and Trond Berntsen. Berntsen was actually an officer in the National Police Immigration Service but was on the island as a security guard. He had performed this function every summer for the past twenty-five years.

At 5:21 p.m. the first shots were fired in front of the Main Building down by the quay. The perpetrator continued up the hill toward the Cafeteria, killing one person on his way. In the square outside, three more were shot. Several people standing nearby and others inside the dining room witnessed the murders, and panic broke out. On the south side of the Cafeteria he shot two more. There were also many witnesses to these murders, both from the campground and from inside the main hall of the Cafeteria building.

After shooting around the campground, the terrorist entered the small hall of the Cafeteria. There were still a great many people in here, and chaos ensued as everyone tried to escape at the same time. Several were injured jumping out of the windows. Thirteen young people were killed in the Cafeteria building, and many more were physically and psychologically damaged for life. This is the one place on Utøya where you can still see physical traces after the terror attack.

Since the Cafeteria was the scene of thirteen brutal murders, it wasn't easy to envisage it again functioning as a meeting and gathering place, kiosk, and dining area. This was also the reason that the AUF had decided that the building should be demolished. However, for many of those affected and bereaved, the small hall, great hall, and corridor had already become sacred sites, places to commemorate those who were killed there, and nothing else.

Various people therefore argued that the building should have a conservation order, or at least be left unaltered. Others feared that actual conservation would mean that the building, and thus the whole of Utøya, would be frozen in time as the crime scene it became after the terrorist's horrific actions. Many people thought that a solution such as this would make it impossible to use Utøya as a political camp, thereby effectively finishing the terrorist's work for him. Several of the bereaved made it clear that they didn't want the building used for any new activities, but neither could they bear the idea of it standing as a symbol of death and destruction. It had to go, they said.

The situation was completely deadlocked. Some would have to "lose" for others to "win."

All the other places around the island where victims were killed were out of doors. Nature itself took care of these; life went on by itself. Flowers bloomed, wilted, and bloomed again. Wind, water, and weather shaped the environment in their own manner, at their own speed. Inside the Cafeteria building, time stood still in a completely different way. Only man-made changes would make an impact here.

As this was the only building affected, the only indoor area where people had died, it posed a particular dilemma. How we handled the Cafeteria would come to symbolize how we handled the island as a whole. Even many of the bereaved who hadn't lost their loved ones here were deeply concerned about this building's future.

Difficult phone calls

How could we find solutions faced with a situation like this? How could we acknowledge and respect the emotional wounds of the survivors and the victims' families? How was it possible to reconcile at times totally opposing views and interests, or different conceptions of time?

How should we facilitate proper, constructive dialogue about the future of a place struck with terror? A dialogue between people who had lost their loved ones and were in the middle of a crushing process of grief. How was it possible to create anything meaningful out of something so meaningless?

Even though the support group had asked their members to express their opinions about the future of Utøya, there was no doubt that we had to dig deeper than this to ascertain the thoughts and needs of those who were directly affected by the events. It was necessary to find out what was required in order to create a meaningful future for the island, and what could be done specifically to meet the needs of the Utøya stakeholders. It also became clear that we needed to create arenas other than large meetings to facilitate this meaningful dialogue. With feelings running so high, it was practically impossible to have thoughtful, constructive conversations in large gatherings.

This heralded the start of a demanding but extremely important period of work. The goal was to establish a good dialogue with at least one representative of each bereaved family. To do the same with all of the 495 survivors would have been impossible, especially with the resources we had available (basically me), so with them we simply had to communicate via the organizations they belonged to: the AUF and the support group.

As a result, I never had as close contact with the majority of the survivors as I did with the many bereaved. Most of the in-depth conversations I had were through the AUF and during meetings with the support group. Unfortunately, it's not inconceivable that this gave me a distorted impression of the survivors' views, but I was obliged to prioritize the families.

So where should I begin? I contacted the authorities, both the Ministry of Health and Care Services and the Ministry of Justice and Public Security, to ask if they had contact lists of those who had died and their families. They didn't, or none that they wanted to share with me at least. The support group couldn't help me either. Therefore I had to compile my own list, by means of trial and error. Search online, read newspaper articles, find out who the parents were. Then use a directory to find their phone numbers.

It was important not to make any mistakes here, so I spent a lot of time on preparations. I have since learned that the Labor Party had almost complete, albeit unofficial contact lists. Just why they never gave me, or the AUF, access to these lists remains a mystery.

I had the names of the dead and a little information about them, but I needed their date of birth. This was one of the first things that occurred to me when I was compiling the list. Nothing could be worse than calling the grieving parents on the birthday of the child they had lost. I googled some more, and gradually added each victim's date of birth to my calendar. This way, I could see when it was safe to send out messages or call the parents. We thus avoided any public communication on these dates. Never a status update, never an interview, never anything in the media on the birthday of one of the dead.

Before I started to make the calls, I needed more information. I couldn't phone without knowing anything about the murder victims. I began by finding out where and how they died. Every single one, place by place. I read the verdict and scoured books. When I went to Utøya around this time, I visited the places where the police had found the victims, and I tried to piece together the sequence of events. Bolsjevika, the Pump House, Stoltenberget, the hillside, the Path of Love, the southern tip of the island, the steep slope, the Cafeteria building. I read the notes from the trial, the descriptions from the autopsies. Autumn and winter. Silence, death, and pain.

On many occasions I wondered if this was all really necessary. Because it was tough immersing myself in all that incredible brutality and intense suffering. However, I was going to spend a lot of time on what I hoped would be intimate, important conversations—so I had to have some background knowledge, not least about the different parts of the island that would certainly be significant during many of these exchanges. I had to know about, sense, feel some of the pain that inhabited these places. It wasn't my job to be a psychologist, priest, or friend. I was going to discuss the future of the place where the families' loved ones had been murdered. The least I could do was gain some insight into what these painful places meant for the bereaved, and how gruesome the attack actually was.

Eventually I had compiled a detailed, systematic dossier on each of the victims. Now that I had the parents' (or who I assumed were the parents') names, phone number, and address, it was just a question of getting started. But it wasn't that easy; I dreaded picking up the phone. If it had been a one-off polite conversation or a message of condolences, it probably wouldn't have been so demanding, but I was about to start a dialogue on such a terribly difficult subject. I often sat there for several minutes just staring at my phone before I went ahead and called. What could I expect at the other end? How would this call help? Was it a good time to talk?

In many cases it's the parents who are registered as owning the phone numbers, while it's the children who use them. Several times when I called, it was a child or teenager who answered the phone—probably the victim's brother or sister. They shouldn't have to deal with the plans and future of Utøya, and certainly not with me. For this reason I never introduced myself as Jørgen from Utøya when I rang, just Jørgen Watne Frydnes. As soon as it was clear that I had come to the right person, I explained who I was and why I was calling.

The opening of the phone conversation was the most difficult part. "Hi, I'm calling to discuss the future of the place where your child was killed." Because actually that is what I was doing: calling them in the midst of their mourning.

Would the conversation simply add to the burden of grief they were carrying? Would it help in the slightest? Were we doing this just to be able to claim that we had spoken to all the bereaved? Perhaps it was better to reach them in other ways—by letter, email, face-to-face? I kept finding one excuse after the other and put off calling from one day to the next. And then another week. But the debate about Utøya's future raged on—in the media, within the support group and the AUF, on social media, nationally and internationally. And it wasn't a healthy debate either. Come on, Jørgen, just pick up your phone and make those calls!

I began by calling the people I had already talked to at the support group meetings. Rumors that someone was phoning the families spread quite fast. After a while, the bereaved were expecting a call when I rang, which made it easier to start the dialogue.

The first conversations were mostly about establishing a direct line to those of us working with Utøya. It was the first occasion for the families to express their opinions directly to us, one to one. There were many challenging but useful exchanges.

Those plans that were presented in September, they were bloody outrageous.

The AUF have already made up their minds. Why call now?

We'd like Utøya to be a park, with all the money raised going to its upkeep. Can't imagine the AUF camp being held there again. Wish I could be more constructive, but I just can't handle it right now. I'll call back when I'm up to it.

Thank you so much for calling. It's really positive that you've got in touch, but this is a matter for the AUF to decide themselves. Just don't let terrorism win. Don't give up.

We'd like there to be a peace center and memorial. Not a summer camp. The idea of reclaiming Utøya is more important than all the other sensible arguments. Try to see it from our point of view.

Keep the Path of Love as it is. We need to be able to sit where our child was killed. Not very often, but a few more times.

We're not happy that the Cafeteria building is going to be demolished. Time will pass, and we keep changing our minds, but it's still hard to imagine there being any activity on Utøya again. No earlier than 2015, preferably in five years, but hard to say. We were adamant about this just a few months ago, but things might change with time.

We are definitely against demolishing the Cafeteria building and the Pump House. In our opinion, the Cafeteria is a memorial.

Really looking forward to the AUF using the island again, and we want it to be rebuilt. What happened in 2011 mustn't stop things happening in the future.

Great that political activity will continue. Don't see anything wrong with things starting up in 2014. But it's important to keep the Cafeteria. At least let parts of the building remain or be included.

Put the plans on ice for five years and have a good think. The presentation of the plans has further messed up our grieving process.

The commemoration of the anniversary was a disaster. Visiting Utøya is important for the process of grief—laying flowers, lighting candles—so it's incredible that the AUF simply closes the island to us.

We really appreciate talking to you directly, one to one, not just via the support group.

Please keep the piano in the small hall.

Traumas and inconsolable grief

I wade over to the campground. It takes time in deep snow. The area of grass we can skip across in the summer, trailing our toes through the flowers, is now difficult to negotiate. The cold keeps life at bay, pressing it down under the dense snow. I make my way to the outdoor stage at the campground. There's no music here now, just complete quiet.

In the beginning of the process, this was a heavy silence full of dark thoughts. I spent the early days immersing myself in the most painful aspects of it all, the places where the victims lost their lives, the way it happened. But was it right to only be preoccupied by this? Of course it was natural, but was it right?

For myself and many others who didn't have their own memories from the fantastic days on Utøya—the beautiful summer days with friends and lovers, an island bathed in sunshine and political engagement—it was natural that the 2011 terror attack set the tone and provided the primary association. Standing here by the stage in the middle of winter, with an icy wind biting my face, it's often the discomfort that I feel more than anything else. The trees are weighed down by heavy snow. It's beautiful, but harsh and threatening too. The ice cracks. Hearts are broken. The stories I know from the stage, on the other hand, are all about the opposite: about July 21, joy, music, and friendship.

"We must remember and celebrate them for how they lived, not how they died." It was someone from the AUF office who said these words during a discussion one lunchtime. Until then, I had spent a lot of time reliving the victims' final hours. I had been concerned with the dramatic end to their lives. Yet this comment from one of the staff, who was also one of the survivors of July 22 on Utøya, opened my eyes. Who were they? What did they stand for? What were they passionate about? I couldn't pretend to know those who died. I hardly knew anyone in the Workers' Youth League, and no one that had been at Utøya on July 22, 2011. At this point I barely knew the island. But I had to show the parents some respect by at least knowing something about their loved ones. From that day I spent much more time finding out who they were and how they had lived.

I added a short text to my calendar from the eulogy for every single victim that was read aloud at the trial. This was a good way to get to know them, while also reminding me what my job was actually all about. I searched online for information about where they were from, what they were into, why they had been at Utøya, their family situation, and so on. I read news stories, tributes, and Facebook pages over and over again, and slowly but surely, I caught a glimpse of sixty-nine people's lives.

The weeks passed, and I went further and further down the list. After contacting thirty or forty families, I felt I had already made some progress; the work was useful and meaningful. But I was only halfway. The number of people concerned was overwhelming. The tragedy had affected so many. Time and again I felt discouraged. How could I bring myself to contact them not just this time but also to follow up with them properly afterward? It was tough preparing the phone conversations. It took time to dial the number, but I was always glad I had done it afterward. I was making headway.

Still, talking on the phone can never replace meeting face-to-face. Only then can you really go into depth, explain, and understand. A natural way to follow up on the phone calls was therefore to try and meet the families, one by one. If we had been a public body or had unlimited access to the resources we needed, reaching everyone probably wouldn't have been a problem. But we weren't a public body, and I was the only one doing this job.

One of the first meetings I had was in Halden, a small city in southern Norway. What would the bereaved say? How would they act? How could I remain polite and sensitive and at the same time be constructive and specific? Freddy and Marit lost their daughter on Utøya. Elisabeth was killed in the great hall of the Cafeteria building. Her sister, Cathrine, was also on the island. Cathrine was shot several times but survived, after hiding among dead teenagers on the steep slope below the Path of Love. I met them at a café. They were skeptical about the AUF returning to Utøya and very negative about demolishing the Cafeteria.

They certainly didn't mince their words when we talked together. It was tough hearing about their grief and suffering, and the anger they felt toward the AUF. Some of their comments were fair, others were unfair, but everything was understandable. Our meeting also gave a face to the sorrow and experiences I had previously only heard about, and an insight into the family's personal challenges. They said how they felt about their dealings with the police, the Norwegian Labor and Welfare Administration, the political establishment, the AUF, hospitals, lawyers, and the media—both at the beginning and later on. All of this shaped their views on Utøya's future.

In the midst of a difficult situation, I could only make a small difference in matters regarding the island. They told me how distressing they found the discussions about Utøya. They explained how vital it was not to pull down the Cafeteria; all that horror couldn't just be swept underneath the carpet. All I could really do was listen and thank them for their important remarks. But I couldn't promise any changes as the AUF was going to discuss the plans again among its members. It was frustrating not being able to promise anything at all.

I was to have many such meetings in the course of the next few months—at a family's home, at a café, or somewhere else. Face-to-face. Looking through photo albums, at pictures of teenagers no longer with us. Hearing about pain and grief. Anger and frustration. Discussing Utøya, in general terms and in detail.

I had lots of cups of coffee and lots of important conversations. Halden, Larkollen, Årnes, Toten, Orkdal, Trondheim, Hommelvik, Bardu, Oslo, Bærum, Bergen. South to north, east to west. I met many exceptional people. Some of them were understandably angry, while others welcomed me with open arms.

I have traveled alone during the civil war in eastern Congo. I have been robbed at knife point in Egypt. I have skied down sheer mountainsides in the Alps, fed wild hyenas in Ethiopia, helped children wounded by artillery fire and in acute need in Afghanistan. Nevertheless, meeting these people for the first time to discuss Utøya was still one of the scariest things I have ever done. I had no training in this; I was an amateur. I am not particularly fond of small talk, and I am not much of an extrovert either. The first few minutes I simply had to focus on breathing and behaving normally. I would get a sense of the atmosphere, waiting for tensions to ease. There was a lot of blunt, harsh feedback well into the visit, once trust had been established. It was the beginning of the conversation that was the hardest part. There are many things you can say at such times that actually make the situation worse, but there are very few things you can say to make it better.

"What I can't stand is when people that weren't there say they understand what it was like. But there's no damn way they can understand. Not a chance in hell." I kept hearing this, or something similar, from the AUF members who had survived. I suppose they told me this in order to explain, to argue against the know-it-alls out there who both in private and public had criticized and condemned the actions of some of those who were on Utøya that afternoon. However, they also said this as a kind of warning: Don't try to pretend you understand, don't pretend you know. Listen to us, listen to our version, talk directly to me—don't interpret things and act as if you understand.

I realized early on that it was necessary to seek professional help in order to improve the quality of the process we had started, so I reached out to Norway's leading experts in trauma therapy. They provided me with a lot of advice and tips that proved useful as the work progressed. One very useful, concrete suggestion was to avoid any unnecessary contact, information, and discussions during the festive season. In addition to the period around July 22, Christmas is the worst time for many families. The empty place at the table on such occasions is all too obvious.

I learned more about what trauma reactions teach us about fundamental psychological processes, about both vulnerability and posttraumatic growth. We also talked a lot about what trauma can do to us in its most basic form. Unfortunately, this was something that I could relate to. I will never be able to understand what it was like on Utøya that afternoon in 2011. However, if you have ever had a traumatic experience, you can to a certain extent relate to other people's feelings, their chaotic thoughts, and explanations of irrational acts.

In 2010 I was traveling around Ethiopia and Somaliland, two wonderful countries in the Horn of Africa. Most people probably aren't very familiar with Somaliland. It's the northwestern part of Somalia, but the area functions as a de facto independent state. Somaliland declared its independence in 1991 after being in a voluntary union with the rest of Somalia since 1969. Prior to that it was a separate British colony, whereas the rest of Somalia was under Italian control. For the last twenty years, the country has been a glimmer of democratic hope in an otherwise less than democratic part of the world. No other country has yet recognized Somaliland, but even so. Although they have both history and international law on their side, realpolitik prevails in the case of Somaliland. There are beautiful beaches in the Gulf of Aden; the diving and snorkeling in the Red Sea along the world's second biggest coral reef is unforgettable. The place has deserts, mountains, and a fascinating culture—plus terribly boring food. In many ways it's a fabulous, interesting country, but it also faces considerable challenges.

I was walking around the outskirts of the Port of Berbera with my British traveling companion. When traveling between towns in Somaliland, you have to have an armed escort for security reasons, but this doesn't apply inside the towns themselves.

On the way back to the town center we met a group of young men. Although they didn't speak any English, they clearly wanted us to give them our cameras. I had a large reflex camera in my backpack, while my British friend had a cheap little camera he could more easily part with. As he reached for it, however, he was struck hard in the face. Bleeding profusely, he handed over his camera.

This wasn't the first time I had been robbed on my travels, so I felt the situation was still relatively manageable. The men continued to behave in a threatening manner. We started to walk slowly backward, asking them to calm down. Without a common language, though, this didn't really help.

More youths soon came running out of a big building at the top of the hill a few hundred meters away. Their shouting further whipped up tensions. Realizing that we had to get away as fast as possible, we made a run for it. Shortly after, we turned around to see if they were there. Several of them were charging after us, yelling and screaming, and they were armed.

"Run!" I shouted, and as I turned back around I heard the first shots. Then there were more of them. The sharp sound of machine gunfire, bullets hitting the ground around us. Clouds of dust, utter panic.

I have never sprinted so fast in my life. Wearing sandals, we fled in desperation over the sand, stones, and thorns toward the town. We kept running, driven on by pure panic and adrenalin. My body reacted all by itself, my reflexes took over. In the distance we saw a truck coming toward us. My first thought was that help was on its way. My second was that they were accomplices. We hid behind some bushes.

Although we had come quite a long way from the men who were firing at us, we were still panic-stricken and full of adrenalin, so it was hard to talk calmly about what we should do next. Even so, we quickly agreed to remain hidden until the truck had driven past, then continue running back into town to find our hotel. That was where Abdi was waiting, the armed guard we were traveling with, and who would at least be able to help us.

It was getting dark. We couldn't quite see if there was still anyone following us. The minutes it took for the truck to drive past seemed endless. We were both convinced we were going to die—here, in the middle of the desert, in no-man's land, with a gang of armed youths chasing us.

We could just make out the lights from the town and what we were sure was our hotel. We decided to walk the last bit, behaving as if we were normal residents out for a stroll. Terrified, we sauntered back to the hotel. Exhausted and dripping with sweat, we limped inside. Abdi and the hotel staff were shocked by the sight of us: two young Western tourists covered in thorns, blood, and vomit, obviously distressed, so worn out that we could hardly manage to explain what had happened. Blood mixed with sand and dust formed a small reddish-brown puddle around our feet. Since fear overshadows all other emotions, I didn't notice the exhaustion and pain. We drank some water and gradually calmed down. Then we sat there pulling long thorns out of our feet and tending to our injuries.

It wasn't long before the gates of the compound suddenly burst open. A large cloud of dust formed in the backyard and in came a convoy of big Toyota Land Cruisers. Out jumped a load of soldiers, who dragged us to separate corners of the hotel area and sat us down on chairs. No one spoke English, so we had no idea what was going on.

The more I tried to explain and ask what was happening, the worse the atmosphere got. The soldiers yelled louder and louder. The sweat ran, the frustration grew. One of the hotel employees came over. He knew a bit of English and was told to translate what one of the higher-ranking soldiers said. His vocabulary was limited, however. I only picked up words like "spy," "pictures," "illegal." I was worried that anything I said would be totally misinterpreted, so I decided to say as little as possible. This didn't make the commander of the soldiers any happier.

Then most of the soldiers, including the commander, suddenly left as fast as they had come. A couple of soldiers with Kalashnikovs slung over their shoulders remained, though. What now? We weren't allowed to move or talk to each other. We each sat nervously on a white plastic chair, drenched in sweat. Without a word, the soldiers walked off. They sat by themselves with their feet on the table and took out some bunches of fresh khat. One of the hotel staff waved at us, saying: "You can go to your room."

We didn't get much sleep that night. The slightest noise frightened us, and we were suspicious of people walking outside our room. What would the next day bring? At least we were able to agree on our story and devise a strategy before the inevitable interrogation.

The next morning started well. We had calmed down and been given something to eat and drink. The soldiers had left during the night. Sitting out of the burning sun on the white plastic hotel chairs in the shade, we summed up what we intended to do now. Neither of us was especially keen on hanging around any longer than necessary.

Then, out of the blue, the cars from the day before drove back in through the gate. Out jumped even more soldiers than last time. They spread out around the hotel area, checking everywhere they went. Next, an older man in a suit climbed out of one of the cars. We were led over to a table in the middle of the square. Two chairs were waiting for us on one side. The smartly dressed older man was already sitting on a chair on the other side. "You are charged with espionage," said the man, who had a perfect American accent. I felt as though someone had thumped me hard in the stomach.

"Allow me to introduce myself. I am the governor of Berbera, this province. I was summoned by the chief of defense when the local unit of the army reported an incident of espionage."

We both started talking at once.

"Take it easy," said the governor. "One at a time."

As we explained our version of the previous day's events, the governor's knowing little smile gradually turned into laughter. The man exuded friendliness, and his good humor made us relax and trust him.

"What you were told here at the hotel is not correct. The building on the hill you went to photograph is no longer a hospital. It is now a military camp."

The rest of the conversation continued on from this. We had run off after taking illegal photos of a military installation. The soldiers had tried to explain but they couldn't speak English.

"But why did they shoot at us?" we wondered.

"Their orders were clear. They were shooting to stop you."

We were lucky to be sitting there at all. And it was a happy coincidence that the governor was a decent man. We had to apologize in person to the camp commander, who was still furious, but after that it was all over. The governor called the chief of defense, the chief of defense called the camp commander, and then they all vanished.

We continued traveling around Somaliland after this, but the incident had a huge effect on me for the rest of our journey and in many other situations to come.

Traumatic events can leave a deep impression for a very long time. Whenever I consciously or subconsciously remember what happened in Somaliland, my body goes into the same crisis mode, sparking the same defense mechanisms as during the shooting in the desert. A loud unexpected noise, someone who suddenly appears behind me, the smell of dust, the sight of a weapon. My body can still react violently, all these years later. And it can happen even if I am not actually scared anymore, even if there's no reason to be scared.

On Monday, October 3, 2011, Utøya was opened up to the media. Before the press visit I was able to go to the island for the first time. When we were gathered outside the Main Building, there suddenly came a loud, sharp noise. Then came another, and another, more and more. There was no mistaking the way that several of the survivors from July 22 reacted.

"Was that shots? We've got to hide!" someone cried out in fear. The regulars to Utøya knew that there's a rock crushing plant in the hills on the other side and that that is where the sounds came from.

We soon calmed everyone down, and talked about what it was, but also about why the body reacts how it does. The fact that I have had a traumatic experience and genuinely been scared I wouldn't survive has in no way been crucial for my work with Utøya and those affected by July 22. Nevertheless, I think it has allowed me to appreciate more fully what it is like for the survivors having to cope with a traumatic memory for the rest of their lives.

No experience of dealing with terrorism

From the outdoor stage I walk over to the road on the other side of the campground. Both the road and the campground are covered in white today. The snow has settled after a long cold, windy day, and the gray clouds are all the lighter for it. The trees that stood here so lush and green in the summer are now just dark silhouettes of snow-covered branches. Most people know Utøya as a summer island. It's quite different here in the winter.

The road is known as the E6. I have never managed to find out why exactly, but the most plausible explanation has no doubt something to do with how the AUF organizes its camps. There's a long-established custom that the various county branches occupy the same place year after year. The road crosses the campground, thus the counties, from south to north. Just as the real European route 6 goes through six of Norway's eleven counties, the E6 on Utøya crosses the same counties on its way from the Schoolhouse, across the campground, to the Cafeteria and the hillside.

No one else has walked along this road for a while. Today, however, there are two of us here. The American researcher and I trample through the snow and wander around the campground. The snowflakes haven't stuck together yet, so each time our feet touch the ground, a white cloud of snow crystals flies up around us.

We talk about history, July 22, and our process. Like so many others, the researcher is very interested to learn more about this place.

We take a break under the big pine tree in the middle of the campground and stand there in silence taking in the view of the empty island.

"What experience does Norway have with handling events like July 22?" he asks.

"Well, we have a number of memorials, and there's quite a lot to learn from the period after the Second World War, but the July 22 attack came as a total shock. We suddenly had to deal with something completely new."

Norway hasn't needed to establish any routines for handling processes in the aftermath of serious terrorist attacks. This issue has been important for Utøya, and it made us face up to some hard truths early on. A lack of precedents for how to manage places affected by political violence means, first and foremost, that there is no set answer, no Norwegian way of doing things. We have had to find everything out for ourselves. We have had to do what we thought was right based on our own history, culture, and process.

We weren't offered any support, advice, or guidance from society at large or from the authorities. Yet we weren't just left to deal with Utøya by ourselves either, as a lot of different people had strong opinions about what should happen next.

The other sad truth we had to acknowledge was that there are places all over the world that have experienced terrorism. In many ways July 22 is a unique occurrence, but atrocities caused by individuals with evil ideologies are unfortunately all too common.

It became clear to us that we required external expertise on how to best handle traumatic memories. But what kind of help did we really need? During the initial phase, the AUF had had good working partners when it came to construction and process management, architecture, and financing, whereas there had been practically no input concerning the issue of commemoration. In the beginning there were many self-appointed experts in this area—authors, academics, and professors. They knew best and the advice they gave was clear. Preferably in the media, not directly to us.

All of this input had to do with the past, not the present, and certainly not a living future. There was naturally considerable internal concern that we would become too dependent on external expertise. If the advice we received went against the vision we had for Utøya's future, what would we do then?

In the public debate, many people referred to locations targeted by violence or terrorism that have simply become memorial sites and/or places of learning. Places where time stands still. However, we were determined that Utøya would continue to be full of life. Therefore, we needed an expert who also had experience with places that have managed to strike that balance—places that aren't frozen in time but live on with past traumas and new life in peaceful coexistence.

In April 2013, Tor Einar Fagerland gave a lecture to the art committee for memorials after July 22 in which he put the Norwegian process in an international context. Tor Einar is associate professor of history at the Norwegian University of Science and Technology. He is head of the research project "July 22 and the Negotiation of Memory." This project examines the cultural afterlife of the terrorist attacks on Norwegian society. It focuses mainly on how time-specific, permanent memorials are presented and interpreted in our public spaces.

One of those present was the AUF's representative on the committee, Mari Aaby West. Mari was on the executive board of the Workers' Youth League and one of the people I worked most closely with. After the lecture Mari came over to me and suggested that I contact Tor Einar. Thus began a working relationship with him that has become increasingly close. In the course of 2013 Tor Einar introduced the group working with Utøya to more and more research on commemorative processes and the handling of traumatic memories. We learned a lot, and the complexity of such matters became increasingly clear.

In December 2013 I visited Tor Einar in Trondheim while I was traveling around meeting the families who had lost their loved ones. I had visited the bereaved in Trøndelag, and I had met the support groups for the southern and northern part of this county. I had also given a presentation at the Falstad Center. Tor Einar showed me round the town so we could discuss examples of how present-day life coexists with traces and representations of past events.

Falstad, which was used as a prison camp and death camp by the Nazis during World War II, also has to reconcile memories from the past with contemporary needs and wishes. There is, of course, a big difference between the expectations of an ex–prisoner of war from the former Yugoslavia and a class of school students. Should Falstad primarily serve the needs of survivors from the camp, or is it more important that today's younger generation can use the center actively for educational purposes?

One of the many places Tor Einar showed me in Trondheim was at the Museum Square in the city center. The persecution of Norwegian Jews began in earnest in the autumn of 1942. On November 25, thirteen-year-old Cissi Klein was arrested by the Norwegian police in her classroom at Kalvskinnet school. The following year she was deported to the Auschwitz concentration camp, where she died in the gas chamber the day she arrived. In 1997, on the anniversary of the rounding up of Jews in Trondheim, students from Kalvskinnet school unveiled a statue of Cissi outside her home. School students visit the memorial on this day every year.

Another moving story from the dark side of the town's history may be found in front of a pub. In the asphalt outside the pub there's a small brass plate, part of the world's largest memorial project. *Stolpersteine*, literally stumbling stones, measure ten by ten centimeters and are laid in the pavement outside or near buildings where Jews were living when they were arrested by the Nazis or their supporters. There are almost 350 of these brass stones in Norway, and over thirty thousand worldwide. According to Jewish tradition, a person dies twice. The first time is when death actually occurs, as happens to us all. The second time a person dies is when their name is no longer mentioned. *Stolpersteine* help to keep the person's memory and name alive. The stone outside the pub here commemorates David Isaksen. He was a businessman who opened his own shop at the age of twenty-four. Isaksen was arrested in January 1942 and executed in Falstad Forest in March of the same year.

The difference between Falstad and Trondheim is that the Falstad Center is primarily a memorial site, which means that it is able to make priorities accordingly. Trondheim, on the other hand, is in constant development as Norway's third largest city, and today's needs must come first. However, in their different ways both Falstad and Trondheim attempt to commemorate the past and look to the future at the same time. This was precisely what we were trying to achieve on Utøya.

Tor Einar and I discussed the way forward over a pizza. I was sure that Utøya really needed to engage in dialogue with specialists who could assess the dilemmas we were facing. I therefore asked Tor Einar if it was realistic to set up an advisory group of international experts in this area.

"Who do you want?" asked Tor Einar.

"The best," I answered, somewhat naïvely.

Around this time, in December 2013, I wrote a memo to the AUF leadership and the board of Utøya. The memo drew attention to three challenges that we needed to focus on in order to strike the balance we were after.

The first stressed the necessity of not only rebuilding Utøya but also of making it economically viable to run in the long term.

The second was our growing concern—particularly each time we had visitors to the island—that the terrorist's actions, the sequence of events that day and the route he followed, would dominate as the main narrative for generations to come. Without a special place, a clear voice and a narrative that could respond to all the questions, queries, and reflections about the attack, we were concerned that the events of July 22 would be intensified and retold through the perpetrator's actions, and not from the perspective of the AUF and the victims. Visitors tended to retrace the route taken by the terrorist or ask about his movements. It seemed that the positive history of Utøya was being forgotten, as was the point of view of the victims.

The last challenge we highlighted in the memo was that the argument in favor of demolishing the Cafeteria building—thus removing an important part of the island's history and the personal connection for many of the bereaved—was too one-sided. We proposed setting up an advisory resource group of experts who could help us with these specific problems.

The memo led to a lot of heated discussions within the AUF. Some people thought that our suggestions would just further complicate matters. Others disliked the fact that we had only proposed external experts and that we hadn't managed to find anyone people already knew. We argued that these three challenges were demanding, but that they would also provide us with several good options. Furthermore, handling these issues required expertise and experience that neither the AUF nor Utøya's board possessed.

I later explained these objections to Tor Einar. He completely understood such reactions but still wanted us to convince the others that it was the right thing to do. To prove that these experts were not only concerned with the past, as many self-appointed Norwegian experts had claimed when communicating directly with the AUF and through the media, Tor Einar sent me a description of the aims of the working group responsible for rebuilding lower Manhattan after 9/11. It said: "This would be an integrative design, a complex that meshes memory with life, embeds memory in life, and balances our need for memory with the present needs of the living."

This was exactly what we wanted to achieve on Utøya: a whole, a balance, but where the future was still the main focus.

It wasn't long before Tor Einar got back in touch.

"James Young, Ed Linenthal, and Alice Greenwald. They're the best there are," he said.

Trauma and memory studies have in recent years become a major academic discipline in the United States. People have gotten used to handling massacres over there. Several of their public memorial projects have become shining examples. James Young and Ed Linenthal are among the world's leading academics in this field. Alice Greenwald is director of the 9/11 Memorial and Museum in New York. "Alice Greenwald is to commemorative culture what Barack Obama is to US politics," I was later told by an American researcher. Not exactly lightweights, then.

"These are the leading names in their field, and they're the people you want," said Tor Einar.

"What are the chances of getting them on board?" I asked.

A couple of days later I found out.

> I would be honored and humbled to join the group and to contribute in as many ways as you, Jørgen, and the others see fit! James
>> I am delighted and honored to participate in this planning process. Alice
>> I am happy to help in any way I can. Warm regards, Ed

The collaboration was formalized in February 2014. We established a resource group that would not only engage in dialogue with us but would also give specific advice on how to deal with the Cafeteria building and how to gain control of the narrative.

In addition to James Young, Ed Linenthal, and Alice Greenwald, Tor Einar Fagerland joined the resource group too, along with AUF veteran and Utøya historian Jo Stein Moen and architect Erlend Blakstad Haffner. Erlend was also formally responsible for the plans that were presented in September 2012 and therefore represented the link between the process during that first year and the changes and revisions that lay before us.

Although we had read up on what happens to places targeted by terrorism early on, Alice, Ed, and James provided us with more detailed information:

The cinema in Aurora, Colorado, where twelve people were killed in a mass shooting in 2012 was reopened shortly afterward. Virginia Tech in Blacksburg, Virginia, where thirty-three people died after a mass shooting in 2007, was also reopened. At the same time, the Center for Peace Studies and Violence Prevention plus an outdoor memorial were built nearby.

At Dunblane Primary School in Scotland in 1996, eighteen people were killed in the deadliest shooting incident in modern British history. The school was later completely demolished and replaced by a garden in memory of the victims.

At Ground Zero in New York, the whole area has been revitalized in one of the biggest urban development projects the world has ever seen. As director of the 9/11 Memorial and Museum there, Alice Greenwald had in recent years been responsible for dealing with the most traumatic event in modern US history. This has meant dealing with it in a meaningful way for the United States as a nation but also for families experiencing inconsolable grief. In the middle of this sea of new buildings, new ventures, and new life, we also find the memorial Reflecting Absence, designed by the architect Michael Arad. Beautiful architectonic features have transformed the ruins of the Twin Towers into a meeting place for remembrance, either alone or with others. It's a place you can visit, or choose not to visit. This is also the location of the 9/11 Memorial and Museum, which contains accounts of both the horrific and the positive things that happened that day. The museum also holds discussions about political and religious extremism, the causes of the attack, and life afterward.

In 1995 Oklahoma City became the target of what was then the worst terrorist attack on US soil. Right-wing extremist Timothy McVeigh parked a truck loaded with a homemade fertilizer bomb outside a federal office building. The bomb killed 168 people—including nineteen young children, since the building also housed a day care center.

Both Norway and Oklahoma City, which is right in the middle of the American heartland, have had to acknowledge that terrorist acts can affect *us*, not just other people. In both cases, the shock and pain were exacerbated by the fact that those who died were in supposedly safe places—at day care, work, and summer camp. As if all this wasn't enough, the atrocities were each carried out by a homegrown terrorist. It became clear early on that there was strong support for turning the Oklahoma City bombsite into a memorial and that this would be the heart of a large-scale reconstruction of the downtown area. More than three hundred nearby buildings had been damaged by the blast. The following year, 350 group members presented their plans for a place where people could "come to remember those who were killed, those who survived and those changed forever." In addition to a peaceful, dignified outdoor memorial site, they proposed a learning center that would both help to combat extremism and focus on how a day filled with horror and chaos could give rise to solidarity, compassion, and fresh hope.

The Oklahoma City National Memorial and Museum is today a dynamic and integrated part of the city's identity. It is precisely this interaction between a demanding learning-based archive and museum, a tranquil, dignified memorial and thriving city life, that gives the place meaning and relevance even now, so many years later.

Eight years after the Memorial to the Murdered Jews of Europe (Denkmal für die ermordeten Juden Europas) was opened in Berlin, it's difficult for visitors not to be moved by the dynamic interaction between the abstract landscape sculpture above ground and the information center (Ort der Information) underneath. While you must find your own way around the open landscape sculpture using your personal memories and associations, once underground you can literally immerse yourself in knowledge about what people in given circumstances are capable of doing to their fellow human beings.

It became clear during our discussions with James, Alice, Ed, and Tor Einar that we have minimal experience in Norway with these kinds of memorial sites and incidents. Being able to place our processes in a comparable international context helped us to understand just why they were so demanding and why our conversations were so difficult.

This inspired us to find the right solutions for Utøya's future.

I can't do this anymore

Meeting family after family face-to-face took time. So did the many phone calls. Since I was the only one working systematically in this way, and thus had limited capacity, I realized that we needed to reach out with information and receive feedback more efficiently. Not least, we wanted to lower the threshold for getting in touch with us, asking questions, expressing opinions and frustrations. In the end we decided on a text message solution—in other words, my own phone.

In the initial phone conversations I had with the many families, I asked if they wanted to continue the dialogue by text. The majority said yes, so that they could deal with our messages when it suited them. It could be upsetting, for example, to be watching the news with the family and suddenly be confronted with a report about Utøya. If I knew it was going to be shown, I could send a short text in advance to warn them.

It was fine keeping in touch with the families this way and useful when giving information about how far we had come in the process, what was happening on the island, opportunities for visits, suggestions, and other things. But written messages, and texts in particular, are a tricky format. It isn't always possible to be as precise in a short text as in a conversation.

An example of this was when we invited the bereaved to an open day on Utøya. They were told when and where to come, that they could bring guests, and so on. However, I also wrote that many people had expressed a desire to volunteer, to help out with a concrete task so they had something else to think about, and if anyone else was interested then they were of course very welcome to join in.

This made a couple of families extremely angry.

Those of us who have lost children on Utøya are invited to wash away the blood from the island? How can anyone be so sick in the head as to invite us to something like that?!

Precisely because we had this text messaging dialogue, it was easy to contact them directly to clarify what it was really all about. Although they promptly accepted my explanation, this episode just shows how fragile communication was in the beginning.

Naturally, the bereaved were going through an extremely difficult grieving process at the time. Discussions in the media were full of conflicts and accusations, and most of the media did all they could to stoke an already heated debate. TV 2, for instance, called and sent emails the whole spring with the same question:

"Is it true that the AUF is refusing to let the bereaved leave things to mark the places where their children were killed?"

No, it wasn't true. I gave them the same answer every time, but they didn't stop asking. They obviously wanted explosive news stories.

In the summer of 2013, they announced on *Dagsrevyen* (the early evening news) that "the reopening of Utøya has begun!" Earlier that day NRK had been for a visit to ask what would now happen to the island. The journalist was told that we had listened to the advice from the bereaved families and the national support group and had postponed plans to start rebuilding the island for another two years. However, we were then in the process of changing the rotten cladding on the conservatory walls in the Main Building, as the place was falling apart. This was nothing more than essential maintenance work and definitely in keeping with the support group's recommendations. Yet pictures of a carpenter, some scaffolding, and a few nails provided the NRK journalist with all he needed to produce a speculative and totally untrue story. The following day, the journalist conceded that he had misrepresented the story and corrected the headline he had used online, but the damage was already done. The NRK report appeared on the news, and I got dozens of furious messages on my phone.

After a few days of phone calls and texts, I generally managed to clarify the situation and reassure people. In this instance the NRK story was simply false, something those responsible also admitted themselves.

With one family, however, communicating by phone and text messages proved very difficult. They wouldn't accept my explanations whatever approach I tried. I therefore asked if I could visit them to discuss the NRK matter in more depth and our plans in general. Such visits were a good opportunity to get feedback on our process and hopefully make a better impression than what we had so far managed to do by phone.

I got in the car, and a couple of hours later I was there. As usual, I felt rather anxious. My nerves weren't exactly helped by the sight of the father standing demonstratively outside the house, chopping wood and staring coldly in my direction. There was no greeting to be had from him. While the father of the house remained outside the kitchen window splitting log after log, I met the rest of the family inside. After spending a few hours over good coffee and homemade buns listening to many, many suggestions, I felt a lot better than when I had arrived. It helps to talk. Still, there was no mistaking what they thought about the plans to demolish the Cafeteria building.

"We'll be there the day you start pulling down the Cafeteria. Not to see it for the last time, but to chain ourselves to the front of the bulldozer. If you destroy that building, you'll have to destroy us with it. Then there'll be more than *one* terrorist guilty of murder."

It couldn't have been put more clearly. Despite my optimism after talking at length with the family, which was the very basis for moving forward in the process, I had a big knot in my stomach when I got back in the car.

The years 2013 and 2014 were tough. Many of those affected by July 22 faced major challenges in their everyday lives. While some managed to get on with life, a large number struggled hugely with long-term mental and physical health issues. Research from the Clinic for Crisis Psychology showed that 69 percent of the bereaved mothers and 54 percent of the bereaved fathers suffered from what is called complicated grief disorder during this period. Seventy-one percent of the mothers and 61 percent of the fathers met the clinical threshold for PTSD, which had a serious impact on their jobs, education, and social lives. Half the parents were either partly or entirely off work. Over 70 percent reported suffering from one or more severe symptoms of depression or anxiety. It was therefore not surprising that this period was emotionally draining, that our process was slow, and that the conversations were difficult.

While continuing the dialogue I had initiated with the bereaved, I also became a kind of contact person for all those who needed someone to talk to. An average of ten affected people for each of the victims meant that there were about seven hundred individuals directly affected by the deaths on Utøya. Then came almost five hundred survivors and all of their families. In addition to that were the rescue workers, neighbors, and many others in the vicinity of Utøya on July 22, 2011. Altogether several thousand people were directly affected in varying degrees.

I found it relatively easy to tackle the public debate about Utøya and our plans. It wasn't personal, after all. Furthermore, what the general public always commented on were the plans presented back in September 2012. Outsiders knew nothing about what we were working on, nothing about the processes that were underway, nothing about our internal objectives for improving the project. As a result, the patronizing caps-lock rants of internet trolls and know-it-alls didn't particularly bother me.

The feedback from those affected by July 22 was worse. It was especially hard tackling the most negative reactions from the bereaved mothers and fathers because I took these personally. There weren't many of them, but they kept coming.

Just before bedtime my phone would light up on my bedside table, with the text "you fucking traitor" ruining any chances of a good night's sleep. I would sit up for hours, agonizing over how I should answer, how to best handle and follow up bereaved parents able to send that kind of message.

When I opened my inbox in the morning, sometimes there were emails saying things like "you're raping that island—just go to hell" and "it's your fault this grief never gets any easier."

There were certainly a lot more positive comments than negative ones. I received phone calls and text messages saying how important our work was, what a good job I was doing. But as is always the case, just one negative comment has much more impact than ten positive remarks.

On a personal level, my brave mother was battling with cancer. She underwent treatment after treatment, and it was really tough. She would get better, then have a relapse, over and over again.

"It's hopeless, but I won't give up," she said each time.

Then my dear old grandpa died. Tall, stylish Grandpa—once a handsome youth, with wavy hair and a laid-back demeanour; proud of his six grandchildren, always busy in the garden, with that unforgettable stripey stomach after sitting too long in the sun; a former sailor, voted the most cheerful chap in his hometown of Mandal.

I needed to get away from it all. So when I was asked if I would like to join Médecins Sans Frontières on two trips to document the organization's work in Congo and Afghanistan, I accepted, thinking it would be a welcome break.

In Congo we visited HIV/AIDS projects in the capital, Kinshasa. In Afghanistan we were occupied with the running of a hospital serving three hundred thousand people in the district of Ahmad Shah Baba Mina, on the outskirts of Kabul. We met proud people in great need who had been born in the wrong place at the wrong time—people just like us, but for whom life would never be fair.

In Kinshasa we became well acquainted with a wonderful family of three: Vicky, the mother, Jean Baptiste, the father, and their lovely son Godwin. Both parents had HIV/AIDS, but when their first child was born, tests showed that he wasn't infected. Although this isn't unusual in other countries, in Congo it's a miracle. I developed a close relationship with the little five-year-old, and for me he came to symbolize the hope we must never lose sight of.

In both Kinshasa and Kabul we visited tuberculosis wards run by Médecins Sans Frontières. For a long time afterward I suffered from a painful cough, chest pains, and headaches. I finally went to see my GP.

It wasn't hard to put two and two together; my doctor also suspected TB. However, the tests turned out to be negative, so I just had to go home and pull myself together. I wasn't ill.

A few months later I received an email from the MSF office in Kinshasa. Godwin had developed acute appendicitis but hadn't made it to the hospital in time. I was sitting in a small office belonging to the AUF when I found out that he was dead. The news broke my heart. I sobbed, swore, and hurled my keyboard at the wall. So tragic, so unfair.

Alexander from the Workers' Youth League came cautiously into my office and gave me a hug. It means a lot when somebody shows they care in this kind of situation. Yet after it happened I spent less and less time at the

AUF office. They had more than enough to do building up their own organization, creating enthusiasm and political engagement, without having me crying in meeting rooms, reminding them of all the pain and injustice.

I took a step back, withdrew into my shell, and became increasingly isolated working from home.

Even though I didn't go into the office so much, work was just as intense. There were obviously many who were struggling, and many who needed to blame someone or simply get things out of their system. When we are overwhelmed by death, grief, or trauma, it's not unusual to feel a gaping black hole open inside, a hole that was sealed until then. My phone never stopped ringing.

"He held my daughter's head underwater when she tried to get on board MS *Thorbjørn*. He killed her."

But her daughter wasn't dead, she had survived. And she hadn't been anywhere near MS *Thorbjørn* on the afternoon of July 22. The mother who called me obviously needed help. What should I do? To what extent could I get involved in other people's lives? Should I intervene on behalf of individuals who probably required psychosocial follow-up, people I didn't even know?

Many called me late at night, after clearly overdoing the alcohol. With my phone number readily available, it was the perfect opportunity for some of them to unburden themselves. The AUF was a disgrace. The government was useless. The healthcare system didn't do enough. All the money raised for Utøya should be given directly to the bereaved, not spent on new buildings. Stoltenberg should have resigned. I was an opportunist taking advantage of a tragedy; the death and suffering of others had provided me with a job, and I was reaping the benefits.

Nevertheless, one of the texts left a deeper impression than all the rest. It said:

> What you're doing to us now, Jørgen, is what Breivik did to our children. You're the reincarnation of Breivik—you're destroying us.

I often used to wake up at night sweating and panting. When I got the message about "the reincarnation of Breivik," it all became too much. My body couldn't handle it. I felt dizzy and nauseous. I went back to see my GP. I still had chest pains, it hurt to breathe, and I was sleeping badly. After doing some tests my doctor asked:

No Man Is an Island   75

"What's really the matter? What do you do?"

It was all too much, too hard. I often felt that it was time someone else took over. Why was *I* doing this job anyway? I'd had no previous dealings with Utøya or the AUF. Wasn't it more natural that they handled this themselves? Couldn't someone else continue the process now? My girlfriend kept saying that I needed more people to help me, but I always made excuses about why it wasn't possible.

"I can't ask the AUF for more help. They're the ones directly affected—it's much worse for them than for me."

"Utøya can't afford to pay any more people."

There are lots of ways to cope with demanding situations, whether they are professional or private. My way was to take the bit between my teeth and work on myself at the same time. This wouldn't have been possible without my girlfriend's support. "It'll get better, it's just a phase," I kept saying, both to her and myself.

It did get better—eventually. Our process was progressing, and we began to see signs that our strategy was succeeding. I was getting to know a lot of great people, people who were far less fortunate than myself—bereaved families and survivors who had many reasons to be struggling. My personal challenges and feelings were completely insignificant and trivial, I told myself. I couldn't moan and complain to these people. I could always quit, abandon the work we were doing, escape all the pain, but they couldn't. This was precisely why I couldn't say that I'd had enough. When the pain was at its worst, when the challenges were toughest, I had to reach deep down inside me and feel what I was made of. Would I run away—or stay and finish the job?

Out of respect for those who weren't able to evade the suffering and the problems, I decided that I should at least manage to tackle the challenges the job entailed for me personally.

My greatest inspiration in this whole process has been my closest colleague, Jon. Jon has worked on Utøya since the early 1990s and knows the island like the back of his hand. He's tough, stubborn, and a really nice guy. On July 22 he lost his darling Monica, and their two daughters lost their mother.

Monica Bøsei had been Utøya's CEO since December 1991. A couple of weeks after she started in this position, Monica hired a caretaker: Jon

Olsen from Askim AUF. Jon and Monica were soon more than just coworkers, and there was no doubt who ran Utøya once they became a couple. After losing his life partner Jon now risked losing his job and his island, the place he had looked after and built up for over twenty-five years.

"He took our loved ones from us, but there's no damn way he's going to take our island too," was one of the first things Jon said to me.

I have had this sentence at the back of my mind every single day for almost ten years now. Whenever I was exhausted and couldn't face the thought of working systematically through this whole tragedy, it was Jon's words that got me back on my feet again.

"When life is hardest, you have two choices: either lie down on the sofa and feel sorry for yourself, or get up, go to work, and continue making a difference."

Jon is no philosopher or poet, but these simple words say it all. Jon was already back at work on Utøya in 2012. It was a period when there was otherwise little going on here. He was alone. With just the silence, Utøya, and his thoughts. But he still came to work, day after day. How could anyone fail to be impressed and inspired by his determination, will power, and stubbornness?

I just had to get out my phone and get back to work. We could do this.

Commemoration, learning, and engagement

My conversation with the American researcher is interrupted by the noise of a tractor and a white wall of snow. Jon is coming. With the old snowblower attached to the tractor, he's clearing the road from the Main Building up to the campground. There are two routes leading to the top of the island: the old path up the hillside and a somewhat longer road with a more gradual slope forming a big loop, which Jon is on his way up now. The snow flies up in all directions, sticking to trees and clothes. The silence is broken by the sharp scraping noise of metal against asphalt.

"Asphalt on Utøya!" exclaimed Jens Stoltenberg the first time he visited Utøya after the road up the hill had been paved. A long discussion ensued about why on earth we had done this. Many other Utøya veterans had been just as skeptical. If it were up to Jon, all the roads would be asphalted out here, but for nostalgists, this dark tarmac symbolized the fact that Utøya was no longer how it used to be. For the people concerned with the logistics of a campground, nothing beats not having to mop away the mud brought indoors by one thousand campers. Not least, it contributed to the generally improved appearance of the island.

Even colder, and now covered in a layer of white snowflakes, the American and I continue our conversation. We talk about commemorative cultures and managing history, grief and loss, fear and resuming everyday life, architecture, and imparting knowledge. There's no doubt that for the AUF and those of us working with Utøya, realizing that all the memories and stories must come to the fore, not just on Utøya but in society at large, has been a learning and maturation process.

"How we deal with the difficult aspects of history says a lot about a society's values and self-image," said Tor Einar at a seminar we attended.

"The first obligation at places such as Ground Zero and Utøya is to say what happened there. If the rebuilding ignores, overlooks, or seeks to minimize the traumatic history, it will fail."

This was one of the first clear pieces of advice we got from Alice. In an open democratic society like Norway, we must dare to discuss what and how we will remember. How could it have happened? Why did he want to kill so many people? Where were the police? The younger generation isn't scared to ask. And they will ask, even about Utøya. They want to know what happened in order to understand how and why it was able to happen.

The question facing us now was not whether it was the negative or positive side of the island's history that would determine the future, but how we could ensure that both sides became part of this future in a meaningful way. It was a matter of striking a balance between the past and the future, between remembrance and new life.

We had to accept that we would never be able to devise plans that everyone would entirely agree with. I may have been naïve, but I was still convinced that if we did a good enough job we would manage to create something so important and impressive that everyone, eventually, would be proud and pleased. Slowly but surely we kept getting closer to a solution we believed in. It was discussed by the Utøya board, with the AUF leadership and the board of the national support group.

In the end it boiled down to just three words: *commemoration, learning,* and *engagement*. Three equally important pillars, one not possible without the others. Words that were reflected in the actual building projects.

Utøya would always be a place to remember those we had lost, a place to learn from our history. Yet it would also be a living place that was forward-looking, that with its background and memories encouraged young people to participate, just as Utøya had already been doing for decades.

Past and future. Seriousness and enthusiasm. Reflection and activity.

Our aim was to create this balance for future visitors, not just physically in terms of buildings and a memorial, but also in terms of the feeling you are left with afterward. Utøya could then be an important, dignified place for the bereaved, survivors, and others affected by July 22 as well as for new generations of teenagers attending the AUF summer camp or the various educational activities.

But would this work in practice? Would we be able to explain our intentions for the whole of Utøya with the three words *commemoration, learning,* and *engagement?* If so, how would people respond?

After largely achieving our objective of talking to at least one representative from each of the bereaved families over the phone, we then focused on meeting as many as possible in person. My travels around the country therefore grew more frequent and extensive.

This was important as I now had more and more to talk about. I still had to listen and understand, but I now also needed to find out whether the three pillars for Utøya we had decided on were right for the families, too.

The message I now brought with me on my visits was far more concrete than before. Utøya would be a memorial site, a place of learning and engagement. We often used a reference that was familiar to many: New York. While there were major differences between Utøya and New York, it was useful to refer to something specific that many people knew about. In their own way, they had worked for and achieved a three-part solution in New York, too.

The vast majority of the bereaved and survivors that I met *wanted* Utøya to be full of life and enthusiasm again.

Although July 22 was an attack on democracy and Norway, it was above all a carefully planned political attack. The terrorist's goal was to make Utøya's history as a democratic powerhouse exactly that—history. He wanted to stifle recruitment to the AUF and the labor movement. The terrorist would not achieve his objective. This fundamental principle, the big picture, was brought up over and over again.

Some people still thought that it would be impossible to come back to the island. However, the nature of the discussions changed. We stressed that it couldn't be the same Utøya that the youth returned to. The island *was* different. The idea was to reopen the camps, but within a context that gave the painful history of Utøya its rightful place, where the memory of the victims was never forgotten.

Most people now saw our plans in their entirety. They clearly differed from the ones presented in 2012—as did the response.

My travels up north

In the spring of 2014 I went on a little tour of northern Norway. I had arranged with several families that I would visit them and listen to their views on the future of Utøya. I went to Oslo airport, flew to Bodø, and then on to Andøya. From there I rented a car and started my trip around the counties of Nordland and Troms.

I had driven for an hour and a half, first through the extensive marshlands of Andøya to Hinnøya, mainland Norway's largest island, then to Sortland. As I left the town behind me, heading for the open sea, I received the first text message.

Sorry, but we can't face meeting you after all. It's too upsetting.

For many of those affected, and especially the parents who had lost a son or daughter, it was painful to talk about Utøya. *Too* painful, even. Particularly when the conversation was mainly about the future of the place, a conversation they would rather not have. It was often only one of the parents who could bear to see me. The other one would go out for the duration of my visit, or sit in another room, on another floor.

Every single time I felt so uncomfortable knowing that my presence, my conversations with them, was so distressing that someone had to leave the house, to get away from me. It was tough but understandable, and I just had to accept it.

At first I was rather relieved when the family canceled. I dreaded these visits. I had to avoid saying anything wrong, avoid making people angrier than they already were, avoid leaving the families in a worse state than before I arrived. It made everything easier when the families themselves refused to meet me. So much could go wrong. However, once I had given it some thought, my relief was overshadowed by disappointment. Each visit required a lot of planning and research. It was a unique opportunity for getting vital input on how we should move forward, but also for giving every family an insight into our thinking. Each individual visit was therefore important. All the same, I could only answer that it was fine, that I could come back some other time when they felt ready, or we could speak on the phone.

I decided to take a break, left the main road, drove down to the fjord on a narrow country road, got out of my car, and sat down on a bench. I would have liked to have taken a dip, gone for a walk, or relaxed in some other way, enjoying the beautiful surroundings I was in. But I had to concentrate on the upcoming visit, the conversation we were about to have.

After a while I sent a text message to the next family I was going to visit. They immediately replied.

I never thought you would actually come all the way up here. Unless you've come to tell us that Utøya will be a conservation area, you can just forget it. You're not welcome.

I swore out loud. Another chance was ruined. I answered that it was important and useful for us to meet anyway, but that was out of the question for the family. Once again I had to remind myself that they had their reasons for canceling our meeting. These conversations with me were stressful. At the same time, I had to bear in mind that I wasn't doing this job for my own sake.

I had a long journey ahead of me, with more people to see. I got back in the car and continued northward.

I drove past fishing villages, along winding coastal roads with the thundering ocean on one side and steep green mountainsides on the other. My next visit wasn't until the following day. I had several hours' driving to do and needed to find somewhere to spend the night on the way.

After supper and some more hours in the car, I found the perfect place to sleep. As with other trips I had been on, I had taken a tent with me. With the fantastic scenery northern Norway has to offer, it's better to sleep in a tent than at a hotel.

The next morning the sun finally rose above Spanstinden, the highest mountain in Lavangen and southern Troms. I made myself some coffee on my Primus stove and watched the sunrise from my sleeping bag. Moments like this have been high points in my work these last years. But it wasn't the scenery I was here for; it was the conversations with the families. I had come here to listen—not to the waves in the sea, but to traumatic experiences and difficult dilemmas.

After a quick dip in the icy fjord, my head was ready for a new day. It was still a long drive to reach the first family I was going to see. As the bends in the road sped by, I spent the time mentally preparing myself for these meetings as best I could. The various people I was going to talk to had different backgrounds and experiences, completely opposing views. I went over it again and again while I drove: What was I going to say?

My first visit of the day ended up as a solitary breakfast at a petrol station. Another last-minute cancelation. They couldn't face it. Should I have been clearer about these meetings? Should I have prepared them better? Had the rumor spread that I hadn't handled this well enough, that the conversations didn't lead anywhere?

I started to feel discouraged, yet there were still several visits left. I sent the next family a message to confirm that our meeting was still on, and finally I got a positive answer. I had two good visits that day. I listened to their frustrations, anger, and grief. They understood that it was difficult but said that Utøya shouldn't be closed down. A great many families have insisted on certain principles regarding Utøya's future: Don't let terror define how we live our lives, use the places around us, or shape who we are. Reopen Utøya, and encourage values such as tolerance and diversity to grow even stronger.

Although we also talked about where and how to create the memorial, how to handle the Cafeteria building, and what the overall future of Utøya would be like, it was always good to have their fundamental support in principle. It was also important to use these meetings to discuss how the bereaved wanted to be involved moving forward. Some of them wanted their views heard on a range of things; others didn't. Some wanted a lot of information, others were more than happy with my regular status updates by text, while others again didn't want anything but the most essential messages.

Venturing into an open and shifting dialogical landscape in this way resulted in all kinds of experiences. Some people might find it frightening and unfamiliar territory. I certainly did. Often I just stared at my phone for what seemed like an eternity before daring to call someone who had been affected by July 22. On many occasions I just waited in my car before daring to drive the final kilometers to pay a family a visit, because I simply couldn't hide behind rehearsed phrases or superficial opinions.

However, it made a big impression on me to see how the dialogue we eventually managed to create brought strength and inspiration. For me personally but also, I am sure, for many of the survivors and the bereaved, this was a strength that arose from the joy of creating something together with others, a supportive fellowship that provided room for maneuver to find solutions.

In a process where you need to get backing for a project, ask for input, and discuss different views, the difference between facilitating a debate and facilitating a dialogue may seem slight. However, the difference between the two became very clear to me. While in debates we often see each other as opponents, in dialogues we must see each other as partners. In debates we listen to others to identify their weaknesses, which we can then use to attack our opponents or promote ourselves. In dialogues we listen because we need to be interested in what is said, while in debates we often get entrenched in a particular position.

A dialogue is a joint project where the participants create something together. Joining forces can produce better mutual understanding, brand-new insights, or something else entirely. But achieving something new requires openness and curiosity. Uncertainty in debates is often viewed in a negative light. In dialogues, on the other hand, uncertainty is part of the process. In a dialogue we simply have to be open-minded. No certitude without hesitation. Getting the families to engage in this dialogue, and in this uncertainty surrounding the difficult choices, became a crucial part of my job. It was therefore especially moving and meaningful that so many families, in the depths of their grief, still opened their homes and welcomed me, choosing to join in the dialogue rather than getting embroiled in arguments and debates.

I soon needed to return the rental car back to where my journey had begun, on the island of Andøya. Even though this little trip had been both disappointing and positive, I continued on my journey knowing that those I had met had been given the chance to voice their opinions and hear what we had to say. The ones who had canceled this time would perhaps want to see me later on.

The last leg was to the most beautiful place in the whole of Norway: Senja. With the steep and stunning cliffs behind us, the ferry from Gryllefjord chugged out into the waves. One trip was soon over, but there were many still to come.

Conflicting wishes, impossible choices

The American researcher and I leave the white pine trees at the campground and walk over to the Cafeteria. My fingers are so frozen that I have problems unlocking the front door. We enter the old hallway. It's cold in there too, but a different kind of cold.

There is no mistaking the fact that this building belongs to the labor movement. Old wooden trade union posters still hang from the walls, as do the Labor Party's campaign posters from elections in the 1930s: "Lay down your weapons. The Norwegian Labor Party." The rooms are old-fashioned, rather shabby. The white paint on the walls has started to peel off in some places. Underneath is first the original dark brown cladding, then pale brown paneling, and then white boards have been mounted on top.

Hundreds of children used to come to holiday camps here in the 1930s, and thousands of enthusiastic AUF youngsters have come since 1950 and up to modern day. There are photos of Prime Minister Gerhardsen from the 1950s, volunteers working on Utøya in the 1960s, modern, diverse AUF youth from the 1990s, campground cuisine post–year 2000. The first few meters of the hallway is where the oldest pictures are found.

We go further in. Along the wall on the vinyl floor lie some dried flowers. There are a couple of grave candles in one of the corners. There are many holes in the walls. Bullet holes. No bigger than a few millimeters, but they speak volumes. The lighting at the end of the hall is poor. The only light comes from the lightbulbs in the toilets. Where there was once hope there is still light.

"What have you decided to do about the Cafeteria?" asked a mother sitting at the back suddenly, her voice trembling.

It went completely quiet, as though the air had been sucked out of the room. I had gone to Trondheim to meet the Trøndelag support groups. At this point, the dialogue with the bereaved had only just begun. We had agreed to a change of plans; the time frame had been greatly extended since the initial presentation. The atmosphere at the meeting wasn't too bad, but then came that direct question.

"I don't know," I answered once I had composed myself. "The AUF's decision is still to pull down the building, but we're considering the decision thoroughly from all sides."

"If the place where my son was killed disappears, a part of me will also disappear. You'll destroy an important part of me too. I'll never forgive you."

The meeting was over. I promised to return. I wished I could have promised a lot more, but I couldn't.

On the bus to the airport I thought to myself, Why am I doing this job? It's impossible. How can we ever solve the problem of the Cafeteria building? Whatever we do, whether we demolish or keep it, people will suffer. People who are suffering enough already.

The following week I had a new visit lined up, this time to Larkollen in southern Norway. I just had to brace myself.

"It's very important to us that future generations will be able to see with their own eyes what the terrorist did. And the Cafeteria is the only place where the traces are clearly visible. Our son was shot eight times and died with a number of other teenagers in this building. We think it's totally wrong to raze it to the ground. So I hope you'll respect and honor the dead youngsters by showing what happened to them. If the building goes, it's gone forever."

Jørn and Signe Marie lost their son Bendik in the small hall of the Cafeteria building. I have visited them several times over the years at their home in Larkollen. Even in the midst of their own grieving process, they have always been constructive. They have understood the complexity and different sides of the issue but have always been clear about where they stand.

We have talked at length over homemade buns and coffee. I have tried to understand their needs and explained what other people think—other bereaved families, the AUF, and the experts we work with. It has been astounding to see how many difficult questions they have had the strength to discuss. And it has been a pleasure for me to get to know both them and Bendik, even though he is no longer with us.

We gradually realized that it wasn't necessarily the entire Cafeteria building that was vital to the bereaved. No one had been killed in the dining hall or the kitchen, and there was no evidence of the attack there. It was where their children had died, had last been alive, that was most important to the families. To have a place to go to.

One thing is to see it on television, but to look inside the Cafeteria with your own eyes is an incredibly powerful experience. I think it will be important for posterity. We're already seeing that the public's memory of the Utøya massacre is starting to fade. In the Cafeteria building, visitors can really sense the incomprehensible tragedy of what happened, whether they were affected themselves, they're school students or someone else. Some of the people who were directly affected might not come here for ages. It's impossible to explain what it's like to be here without experiencing it yourself. I really hope they don't tear it down.

Once again I was returning with a clear message. Even though this wish ran counter to the decision that the AUF was still sticking to, it was a relief to be bringing such unambiguous feedback home with me. As I drove back to Oslo after visiting Larkollen, I received a text from another bereaved family:

Don't turn Utøya into a mausoleum. Demolish the damn building. Give new generations the same chance we and our children had—to enjoy this wonderful place and all it has to offer.

Conflicting wishes, impossible choices.

A lot of people, myself included, mainly associated the Cafeteria with death. The bullet holes in the walls gave the various rooms an intense and solemn atmosphere. The silence. The memories. Could the rooms ever be used again?

Renovating a crime scene in order to revitalize it is not an unusual way of handling buildings in the aftermath of terror attacks. Many Utøya veterans, including some leading politicians, made a strong case for doing so. Another alternative when dealing with places that have witnessed comparable tragedies is to demolish everything.

I would often sit alone in these rooms, sensing the significance of the place. Silence can take different forms and bring out different feelings. Living in the age of noise as we do, complete silence can seem like a luxury. Like a meditative or spiritual exercise. Strolling along the beautiful Path of Love or a quiet moment resting on a tree stump in the woods—silence can take this form here on Utøya, too. But inside the Cafeteria building the absence of sounds was oppressive and frightening. I knew full well why it was silent in here, which made it a totally different kind of quiet than nature can give us. The silence in here didn't give, it took. Could we have meetings in here? Could we have discussions? These rooms had provided so much energy, so much enthusiasm, so much hope. But now they were full of something else. Pain, hopelessness. Could life go on in here the way it did outside? No, was my answer every time. Yet the atmosphere in the Cafeteria also helped our thought processes. The quieter it became, the more we heard.

What would happen to Utøya if these rooms weren't here? After sitting by myself on one of the pink upholstered wooden chairs by the old overhead projector, next to the rostrum and the piano, I would often leave the building and go down to the Pump House, where fourteen young people were brutally murdered by the water's edge. Wasn't it enough that that place still existed? Did the Cafeteria, right in the middle of the island, really have to remind us of the tragedy as well? Yes, according to many of the bereaved families and survivors. It was the only place where future generations who hadn't experienced July 22 would be able to see the evil manifested in the walls and floor.

But how could we allow for new life, new tents at the campground, new smiles on the faces of thousands of youngsters in the years ahead, if we let the building stand as it did now? The more I heard from the survivors, the clearer it became that this place was also important for survival and compassion and as an escape route. A lot of people told me how they survived by escaping to the Cafeteria from the campground, jumping out of the windows, then making their way down to the fjord or hiding places around the island. We gradually realized how the various accounts and destinies from different parts of Utøya were embodied in the Cafeteria itself. The same applied to the way the youth had cared for each other that day. After many long conversations with the survivors and the bereaved, it became apparent that somehow or other the Cafeteria building had to be part of Utøya's new life and new identity.

It is the place where my child died that is most important to me.

I lost myself hiding in this loo, I lost my better half and I felt that my life was over. Today I sit here reliving every feeling I had then. Don't take this building with all that I lost away from me.

The bullet holes are the only direct evidence of the atrocity, so they must be kept for new generations.

Almost no one had mentioned the other parts of the Cafeteria; it was the affected rooms that it was important to preserve. Demolishing the whole building would mean removing an important aspect of Utøya's history without it being properly documented. It would also remove the personal link for thirteen bereaved families, the majority of whom didn't want the Cafeteria building to simply be erased from the surface of the earth without any further record of this testimony to the events of July 22. It had to be possible to find a solution somewhere between the two extremes, between total demolition and total preservation.

A less emotional argument, but one that was still raised in discussions, was related to something I actually didn't want to have to deal with: ludicrous conspiracy theories. Conspiracy theories about July 22 were already thriving on the internet, with one theory more outrageous than the next. It was easy to dismiss this as sick people's twisted views of reality; yet if there was one thing we had painful experience of here on Utøya, it was that believing in conspiracy theories can have fatal consequences.

The terrorist's way of thinking was based on conspiracy theories—primarily the Eurabia theory, which claims that European leaders are cooperating with Arab countries in order to "Islamify" Europe. Conspiracy theories spread like never before in today's digital world, and many of them have an effect on our own lives.

On YouTube there are a number of clips, several with thousands of views, spouting theories about the terror that struck Norway.

"The whole thing was staged by the Labor Party itself to get more votes."

"It's really the CIA that is behind the massacre."

"Absolutely nothing happened on Utøya. Everything you've seen in the media is just special effects."

"NATO was responsible because Norway had said we didn't want to continue our involvement in NATO's intervention in Libya."

"It was Mossad, the Israeli intelligence service, that did it. The Knights Templar captured Jerusalem in 1099, the King David Hotel was bombed in 1946, Oslo and Utøya were attacked in 2011. All on the same day: July 22. A coincidence? Hardly. It must be the Jews."

There are many challenges involved in debunking conspiracy theories. The theorists themselves often change their arguments in defense of a conspiracy while still maintaining the same conclusion. In our case, the conspiracy theories wouldn't necessarily be undermined if we simply left the bullet holes in the walls of the Cafeteria. At the same time, the absence of any clear evidence can often be seen as an indication that the attack must be the work of an extremely powerful organization.

Or something like that.

The problems posed by the Cafeteria building produced some constructive brainstorming and led to new initiatives. Polish author and journalist Ryszard Kapuściński wrote that wonderment is a voyage of discovery. For an adventurer, it's mainly all about marveling—at the world, at people, at nature and experiences. Being able to marvel is one of the finest gifts you can have. It is this sense of wonderment that makes me want to travel to unorthodox destinations—and it was this that made working with the Cafeteria a task that we were determined to solve.

However, it wasn't just a question of professional and intellectual wonderment. One of the challenges I faced personally was how to endure the unpleasantness that the conversations inevitably entailed. It was exhausting and extremely demanding to delve so deep into the pain and problems of other people's lives. I wasn't just there to listen but to actually achieve something constructive for the sake of the project. So it was often simplest to end the conversation while we were still on safe ground. Finish before we came to the heart of the matter, the root of any disagreement, the place where emotions really ran high.

It became clear to me that I was using my car to escape from particularly difficult situations. When tempers flared during some of the meetings with the families in their homes, when feelings and the most painful topics took center stage, then I could call it a day, finish the conversation, get in my car, and drive off. After all, I had talked to them and we had made some progress. I made excuses to myself that we had come as far as we could in our dialogue for now. And many times I just left. But I didn't just leave, I fled.

It's quite natural to want to avoid uncomfortable situations. I think a lot of us can relate to that. But it simply wasn't possible for me in this job. It became very clear that I had to get immersed in emotions if I was to gain maximum benefit from these conversations. Because it was when it got emotional that the decisive details came forth. But how could I bear to do so? I had to conquer my fear of uncomfortable settings. My solution on several occasions was to use public transport: to have no car to flee in.

A lot of the families live in remote parts of Norway, a long way from towns and without much access to public transport. When it was two hours until the next bus or train, I couldn't even leave if I wanted to. When we had finished our friendly chat, and when I otherwise might have left, I simply had to stay a bit longer and wait for the next departure. And that is how I forced myself to spend more time on the conversations, on what was really difficult, but also most interesting and constructive. The consequence of enduring the unpleasantness for as long as possible was that the conversation often went much further. Plenty of anger and frustration rose to the surface, but it was often then that the most basic and important insights came too. It was then the photo album appeared, now that we had time to build greater trust. This is how we created a space where we could look to the future, together. Although my escape route had gone, the moment for honesty and intimacy had arrived.

Our American guest opens the door of the small hall and goes out onto the steps. The steps where children attending the holiday camps of the 1930s sat with the lilies of the valley they had just picked; the steps that have been a favorite place for young people to hang out at summer camps over the years—but also the steps the terrorist walked up that fateful Friday. Where the gray steps meet the ground, a white duvet spreads across the campground. The layer of white makes the island seem harsh and cold. But in some places the snow has started to melt. Here and there only small patches remain. Winter never lasts forever. Life changes, the seasons change, people change. We are robust.

SPRING

I follow the wood anemones from the campground toward the Path of Love. There's a small mound here running the length of the west side of the island, separating the path from the camping ground. Tall pine trees dominate this area, dense with branches at the top, bare at the bottom. Between the slender tree trunks, the ground is full of white wood anemones; I leave footprints as if I were walking on snow.

The Path of Love is about a kilometer long and it's at its steepest here in the west. In the spring of 2014, thirty or so dedicated Utøya veterans were set to work here, squatting on their haunches with their hands full of steel wire. A lot of the fences in this area were unsafe, some of them new, some very old, and from the path down the precipitous cliffs to the water it was particularly dangerous. The need to secure the worst sections was urgent. Some of the volunteers hadn't been to Utøya for decades, not since attending the AUF youth camp themselves. Others were parents of survivors from July 22. What they had in common was that they all found comfort and meaning in helping out. Yet for certain people this was a provocation.

We had informed the families about the work that had to be done, and this had generally met with a positive response. One bereaved mother, however, was disappointed and angry. She still could not bring herself to visit Utøya and wanted to see what it had looked like back in July 2011. Luckily she told me about this. It wasn't the whole path she was interested in, just the area along the path where most of the victims had hidden, and many were shot. The simple solution was not to put up a fence here. While six hundred meters of fencing was erected that spring, we left a section of almost two hundred meters untouched. After the mother had visited the island the feedback she sent was clear: "I thought you were just an arrogant, selfish bunch only looking out for the AUF's best interests. That was the impression I got at the beginning. But thank you for waiting for me. We're all dealing with this at our own pace, and I really appreciate how considerate you were to me when there are so many people affected. Next time I come I hope you'll have reopened the island. Don't give up, thank you and good luck." Small things obviously meant a lot to some people, and that's why it was important to remain in close contact. Talk together, listen, find solutions, and create trust.

In February 2014 I became a father myself. The love you have for your own child is indescribable. It's almost impossible to understand before you have become a parent yourself. After baby Aurora was born, I also felt that I changed my approach to the work I was assigned to do. Being responsible for Utøya after July 22 had never been a standard job, but now it became more personal. What if Aurora had been killed? What would I have wanted the people in charge to do? How would I have wanted them to treat me as a father?

Every year the Vestfold support group has invited me to its gathering on the island of Tjøme—a weekend of activities on the coast, with lots of good things to eat and drink. The cities of Tønsberg and Nøtterøy lost three of their beloved girls on Utøya: Benedichte, Maria, and Birgitte. The gatherings with the bereaved from this area have been high points for me in recent years. Beate, Marianne, Terje, Anne, Lizelle, Marte, Stian, Simen, and many more have welcomed me time after time.

When spring came, I was again invited to Tjøme. Although Aurora was only two months old, it was an important event to attend. "Mona and Aurora are of course very welcome to come too," said Beate when she called to ask if I could still make it.

Beate lost her daughter Benny (Benedichte) by the Pump House. Beate is one of the kindest, most generous people I know, but she's also very direct. So we did as she suggested. Mona sat in the sun on the jetty enjoying a cup of coffee, Aurora slept in her pram, and inside the conference room I talked about memorials, our progress, and what we would do about the

Cafeteria building. In the evening, we all had a meal together. Since Aurora was still so tiny, it's an understatement to say that we weren't exactly experienced parents, but the feeling of being part of a big family made it a most enjoyable dinner, even with the odd yell from the baby.

This is the part of the job that has given me a much-needed boost and strengthened my determination. There have certainly been many tough discussions, and a fair amount of unpleasantness has been directed at me over the years, but I have always been overwhelmed with generosity and love.

Resistance from the local Progress Party

In the course of the spring, the lily of the valley slowly but surely takes over from the wood anemone. In May the plant's white flowers appear, dangling from long stalks and surrounded by oval-shaped green leaves. The sun gets warmer, and the flowers stretch toward the light. The forest floor is covered with them.

While the woodland floor of Utøya was being overtaken by the lily of the valley, and we were busy producing actual content for the various projects, we also entered a decisive phase both in terms of the island's future and how the rebuilding process was progressing. On Monday June 16, 2014, the local council in the municipality of Hole was going to discuss the zoning plan for Utøya. It was based on the initial plans presented by the AUF in 2012. We had already significantly modified our concrete plans for Utøya by this stage, but the meeting was just to adopt the overall zoning plan, not to decide what Utøya would be like in detail, conceptually or otherwise.

In the days prior to the meeting, the then mayor Per Berger received a letter from fifteen of the bereaved families asking the municipality to postpone the decision until their dialogue with me and the AUF had made more progress. They asked the municipality to grant them more time. When this became public knowledge on the same day as the municipal meeting was to take place, there was hectic activity among the other affected families. Many were outraged that a small minority was being heard without other people being consulted first.

It was the populist right party FrP, the Progress Party, that submitted the motion to postpone the decision. Any delay would have serious consequences, above all because the wording of the motion was "until the AUF has reached full agreement with all the bereaved." Even though we fully intended to come up with plans that the vast majority would be proud of, it was totally unrealistic to expect unanimity when hundreds of people were directly involved. The wording was tantamount to saying no to reopening Utøya.

The fact that the efforts to stop the plans came from the Progress Party upset a lot of people. The Progress Party was the political party that Anders Behring Breivik was himself a member of a couple of years earlier.

It didn't come as a complete surprise to us that such a motion had been proposed. There was little doubt that the small group in the neighborhood, who also happened to represent the Progress Party on the local council and had taken over the local residents association, wanted to stop Utøya being redeveloped. One of the reasons was that they obviously didn't agree with our work promoting diversity and tolerance, but their anger was probably also a reaction against the controversy surrounding the national memorial at Sørbråten. In their objections to the zoning plan, they listed a number of ridiculous arguments against any further activity on the island. Some people understood certain arguments to be de facto threats, such as the remark that it was easy to find hiding places on the mainland that could be used by snipers in future attacks.

There was no special treatment to be had when the municipality dealt with this matter; in fact, if anything the situation was quite the opposite. Even so, the main challenge locally was the small action group. What they actually wanted, and how important it was to them, wasn't always apparent, however. One of the neighbors who made a complaint against the zoning plan also tried to sell us their property so that we could more easily implement what the plan envisaged for the mainland.

All the attention and commotion caused by this protest felt unreasonable, not least because it was in no way representative. We had had a lot of meetings with the local community, both altogether and with individual neighbors. The large majority said that the most important thing for the neighborhood was that the activity on Utøya should be resumed. They didn't want it to simply remain an island of death; that would make it extremely difficult for local residents to move on, too.

On the afternoon the zoning plan was going to be discussed, my phone kept pinging with texts from infuriated families.

So Breivik needs help from his former Progress Party friends to finish off the job of closing down Utøya for good, then. What can we do to stop the FrP in Hole from delaying the decision tonight?!

This is shocking, Jørgen. The FrP is going to stop any future activity on Utøya. Am I the only one reacting to this madness?!?!

Talking about the terrorist's membership in the Progress Party has become a taboo, both nationally and among those affected by July 22. Any mention of it was seen as blaming them for the terror attacks, so Stoltenberg and the Labor Party chose to ignore the perpetrator's former association with the party. Even though the Progress Party has long been associated with the radical right, they were obviously not responsible for the massacre. But now a lot of people had had enough.

The motion submitted to Hole municipality to postpone the decision was probably met with sympathy by sections of the Conservative Party until shortly before the meeting, and it was the Conservatives that held power on the local council. One of their representatives who didn't support the Progress Party on this matter kept sending us updates on the internal discussions they were having. Would there be a majority in favor of postponing or not? The debate gradually changed direction as dozens of texts from the bereaved and survivors were sent to the mayor's private phone. All contained the same message:

We are directly affected by July 22 and we support new activity on Utøya. Adopt the zoning plan.

Meanwhile, in a meeting room at Youngstorget I sat together with the AUF leadership (Eskil Pedersen, Marianne Wilhelmsen, Mari Aaby West, and Åsmund Aukrust) watching the live transmission of the Hole council meeting. Some of the comments we heard made us want to tear our hair out.

"We greatly respect the bereaved for standing up to the AUF, who want to cover up the bullet holes and remove the blood stains so that their parties can go ahead out there, unaffected by the horrific events."

The way certain local politicians spoke showed little respect for the AUF, the bereaved and survivors, and the plans for Utøya. Yet at the end of a nerve-racking meeting, the motion received just three votes—from the Progress Party's own representatives—and was dropped.

"660 families, representing 1400 people, have said yes to this, so I think a request from 15 individuals is far too small a number for the council to postpone or reject the zoning plan on the table," said the leader of the support group, Trond Henry Blattmann, to the local newspaper *Ringerikes Blad.* Later that evening I got a lot of text messages from survivors and the bereaved, all echoing the same sentiment:

The majority was finally heard today. Together we're going to do this, Jørgen. Utøya will reopen!

Protecting what is most important

With the knowledge that the zoning plan was approved, we continued working on what it would contain. It was still far from clear what our plans were for the island. It was important to reach a decision about the Cafeteria building as soon as possible.

During an intense, productive week in Oslo and at Utøya, where James Young came over from the United States to participate, architect Erlend Blakstad Haffner sketched a solution that retained the central, most affected parts of the Cafeteria (the small hall, great hall, hallway, meeting room, toilets) but removed the kiosk and the dining hall. His sketch on a napkin from Kulturhuset café in Oslo showed the walls in the rooms that were essential to keep for posterity and for those affected. Erlend also proposed building a new structure that would partly protect the preserved areas and partly create a space for future-oriented storytelling, learning, and reflection.

The inside walls of the Cafeteria, the affected areas marked yellow on the napkin, would be kept. The main idea was to remove the parts of the building that weren't vital to preserving the memories from July 22. The outer walls and the rest of the Cafeteria would be taken away. The new body of the building would protect the "sacred" indoor areas, shielding them from the view of the campground right outside.

We could now have a physical place and structure that would house the memories and accounts from different parts of the island on July 22. In so doing, we hoped that the other parts of the island would gradually be free of the events of that day. This made all the more sense because the Cafeteria was the only place where the physical traces from that tragic Friday were actually visible. It also gave us the opportunity to clearly define how the story of July 22 should be told, creating a coherent narrative for visitors in the years to come.

As we had been at Kulturhuset for some hours that day, our table was full of cups of coffee, notes, and sketches. In the middle of all the mess was our napkin, with the yellow lines drawn by Erlend. James, Tor, Einar, Erlend, and I sat there in silence, taking in the sketch. Could this be the solution?

The process from a napkin to a building obviously takes time, but were we finally on the right track? In our enthusiasm we almost ran up the stairs to the AUF's offices on the seventh floor at Youngstorget. "Eskil! Come and see what we've come up with!" I panted. We explained the concept and the thinking behind it. He immediately gave his approval.

The proposal meant abandoning the AUF's previous plans to demolish the whole Cafeteria. It involved keeping the small hall, parts of the great hall, the hallway, and toilets, as well as building a new structure around them. This also meant that we had the area we needed to create a new learning space.

We spent a lot of time discussing this new direction among ourselves and within the AUF. Several members of the leadership and executive board were skeptical. Many people, whether they were in the AUF or not, both survivors and Utøya veterans, were convinced that all the pain associated with the Cafeteria building had to go if life were to resume on Utøya. Whereas in the initial phase we had presented plans and tried to persuade those affected that redeveloping Utøya was the appropriate response to terrorist acts, the situation was now turned on its head. Now we had to convince the AUF itself that traces of the attack should be included on the new Utøya.

A lot of AUF members told me that they were relieved by the proposal. However, I also heard others say how this just proved that "people from the outside," that is, the group of experts and myself, would ruin the Utøya that everyone knew and loved.

We took a long time preparing illustrations, visualizing the plans in their entirety, and arguing that the new proposal would fit with the balance we were after. At one of the meetings where this was discussed, a member of the executive board of the AUF took the floor. Ragnhild Kaski, herself a survivor and subsequently the next secretary general of the organization, said: "What is special about Utøya is that the island contains so much. It contains the very best memories in so many people's lives. And it also contains some of the absolute worst. I think it will manage to contain both." Several others spoke up, talking of their fear that we would forget, but also their fear of remembering. After a lengthy discussion, the resolution to keep parts of the Cafeteria building was passed unanimously by the executive board.

On July 2, 2014, the new plans were presented in an opinion piece and long interview with Eskil in the national newspaper *Aftenposten*. He admitted that the initial plans had been premature, neither well enough prepared nor strongly enough supported by those affected.

When the plans for Utøya were launched back in September 2012, the emphasis was on returning—returning both to Utøya, and for those who survived the attack, returning to normal life. Even though the plans that the AUF presented at the time included new buildings as well as a memorial, not enough attention was paid to the balance we wished to achieve. "The AUF has a responsibility to never forget what happened. We should therefore also preserve the physical traces," said Eskil in the interview.

In the weeks between the AUF's decision to keep parts of the Cafeteria and reports of this appearing in the media, I had spent a lot of time talking to the families who had lost children in the building. We could finally promise them that the affected parts of the Cafeteria would not be demolished after all.

At last I could tell them that there was no question of using the remaining sections of the Cafeteria for normal activities. Instead, we would create a place that the bereaved, survivors, and others could visit.

"Later on there may be a kind of learning center created there too, but it's too early to say exactly what the building will look like at the moment,"

The day before the opinion piece appeared in *Aftenposten*, I sent a text message to all the bereaved. Over eighty different texts to eighty different families. Both the admissions made by Eskil and the new concept itself were largely welcomed by the bereaved and the general public. Those who had doubted our intentions to also preserve the traumatic side of the island's history now felt more reassured. Not everyone was happy, even so.

Several AUF members and survivors were skeptical. How could this function with the campground right outside?

Other families were frustrated that this "house of death," as one of the parents described it, would remain something that they would have to deal with for the rest of their lives. They also feared that this change of plans would lead to further distressing public debates. Others thought we should have better informed them before *Aftenposten* wrote about the decision.

Damned if you do, damned if you don't.

The article in *Aftenposten* was the first time since the autumn of 2012 that we had explained in the media how we had an entire vision for the new Utøya. We had promised ourselves, and those affected, that we would take our time, listen, and learn. It was therefore not right to conduct this discussion in the media. Until now.

We were sure that the plans we had presented were considerably better than our first ones. Gradually, and after input from many different people, they had changed, one step at a time. Nothing symbolized this more clearly than the decision not to pull down the Cafeteria building.

We continued to work on the idea throughout the summer—a building that would protect and safeguard the old one. We called it *Hegnhuset*, a rather unusual and old-fashioned word in Norwegian. A word that required an explanation but described exactly what this building would be like. A new building that would safeguard the memory of those who had never come home, tell the world how they had lived, about their contribution to solidarity and fellowship.

Erlend had suggested that the building should consist of an outer row of 495 posts, one for each of the survivors. All those who were still alive, albeit changed forever, would form a protective ring around the sixty-nine taller and thicker columns supporting the new roof.

One pillar for each of the dead.

At the end of August, Alice Greenwald arrived from New York to help us work on the building project, as well as to take part in the press conference, where we planned to go into more detail than last time. There was still a lot of work to be done before it would be ready, but we were sure that we needed to present our plans to the press for the sake of our process.

The evening before we were to meet the press at Utøya on September 1, 2014, I invited the AUF leadership—Eskil, Marianne, Åsmund, and Mari—to dinner at my house along with Alice and Tor Einar. Eskil announced what his message would be the following day. Suddenly, the underlying disagreement within the AUF over the Cafeteria building resurfaced. Discussions took place during the dinner that I had honestly not expected, about what were the most important considerations and what should be emphasized.

Alice sent me a text on her way home in a taxi. "Are you sure you're in control of the press meeting tomorrow?!"

My answer was brief. "Just leave it to Eskil."

Eskil has received a lot of criticism in the aftermath of July 22. He has been treated terribly by certain bereaved families and others affected by the attack, becoming a hate object for many people all over the country. He is gay, a social democrat, liberal, and proimmigrant. Sadly, that is more than enough for many to hate who he is and what he stands for. Eskil survived July 22 by escaping from Utøya on MS *Thorbjørn* with several others. He has been accused of cowardice, he has been threatened and harassed, and he has had to carry a personal alarm. Those of us who have worked with Eskil have never ceased to be impressed by him. If the smear campaign and all this hate end up depriving him of a successful political career, Norway will have lost one of its greatest talents. There have been many decisive discussions within the AUF of huge importance for Utøya's future, not least whether to demolish the Cafeteria. It has by no means been clear what the outcome of these discussions would be, and I haven't always known what the various members of the executive board have thought about the different issues. Yet I have had a good dialogue with Eskil on every occasion. We have very often been in agreement, and he has supported me throughout this whole process.

So I wasn't in doubt this time either. Even though we obviously had our differences when it came to the details that would be presented to the media the following day, I was sure that Eskil would convey our message clearly and precisely.

We went out to Utøya the next day. We had invited the two biggest TV stations, NRK and TV 2, and a national newspaper to a presentation of our new plans. Inside the great hall of the Cafeteria, Eskil spoke about our process, the history of the building, and why the AUF had changed its mind about pulling it down. Erlend talked about our concrete plans, and Alice provided an international context.

The announcement was featured on NRK, TV 2, and in a number of online newspapers. While it received a good response, many of the bereaved didn't get in touch. I had been expecting to be inundated with reactions, both positive and negative. Hadn't we made ourselves clear? Hadn't our message reached those we wanted it to reach?

We therefore followed up with an opinion piece in *Dagbladet*, written by Alice Greenwald. It went as follows:

> I have learned that it is possible, and also imperative, to find a balance between a return to life and remembering. But I have also learned that the first obligation at places such as Ground Zero and Utøya is to attest to what happened there. If the rebuilding ignores, overlooks, or seeks to minimize the traumatic history, it will fail. I know that a lot of people have found the building plans and the wish to demolish the Cafeteria hard to bear. The new designs for Utøya are now drastically downscaled, and in June the AUF decided, on our recommendation, to preserve remnants of the Cafeteria building. Preserving traces of July 22 inside an unobtrusive, transparent glass building supported by 69 columns will create a communal space right at the heart of Utøya. When young people return to the island, they will find a place that holds the memory of July 22 at its heart, a place where new generations can advance the values that were attacked on July 22. Much work remains to be done on Utøya. We are sure that the AUF will listen to all those affected in the time ahead. We are also sure that we have now taken a big step forward in the challenging process of balancing commemoration and new life.

The immediate response was now huge. I got loads of messages on my phone. "Excellent piece in *Dagbladet* today." "Important decision!" That summer's announcement proved to have even more of a long-term impact. Those affected, as well as newspaper commentators and others, could no longer argue that the AUF and Utøya wanted to erase all the pain. People finally believed that our intentions were good.

I continued working on presenting the plans for Utøya throughout the autumn of 2014, now specifically focusing on Hegnhuset. I again traveled around the country, meeting the support group all together, and those affected one by one.

Once again I visited Signe Marie and Jørn in Larkollen. They were happy with the decision to keep the room where Bendik was killed. We went over the plans together. As they were already familiar with the main points from my texts and the media coverage, we just concentrated on the details. It wasn't until then that they realized the Cafeteria building would only be preserved on the inside. Erlend's sketches revealed that the outside walls were gone; the inside walls drawn in yellow stood alone in the middle of a floor.

"We simply don't recognize the place, and we know the building very well by now. Other people won't understand how it was and what actually happened here. Why have the outer walls been taken away?"

I explained that the idea was to retain the most essential parts of the building, and that keeping these while removing the exterior made the effect all the more powerful. The response was lukewarm. Yes, it was important that the area where Bendik died was intact, and they were grateful for that, but if the room felt completely different, what was the point?

"Can't you do a better job of preserving the interior? Must everything go?"

With the feedback from Signe Marie and Jørn, it was already clear that we would again have to alter our plans. Although Erlend might not want to hear it, we had a lot of work ahead of us. Once more I was heading home from Larkollen after having constructive conversations, but as so many times before—both from Larkollen and many other places around the country where I'd had similar exchanges—I was driving back with even more problems to solve.

We were working with some of the world leaders in their field. Our collaboration worked best, however, when we met face-to-face. We therefore decided to assemble the resource group at Alice's workplace in New York. To get the most out of our week together in the United States, it was vital that I received as much concrete feedback as possible about the Cafeteria building from the bereaved and survivors before we left in October. I needed to have more conversations with them.

In September I returned to Trøndelag, mainly to visit Nina and Steinar in their hometown of Orkdal. Nina's son Sondre was killed in the small hall, behind the piano. The last time we met she said she would never forgive us if the Cafeteria was torn down. We had spoken several times on the phone since then and stayed in touch by text. Now I wanted to talk to them about the Cafeteria building and our plans for Hegnhuset, plus the various proposals for a memorial on the island.

I landed at the airport and had an hour and a half's journey by train and bus before reaching the place where Nina and Steinar live. It was one of those trips where my thoughts were entirely focused on the upcoming visit. I was looking forward to it and dreading it at the same time.

I felt terribly nervous as I got off the bus. Steinar picked me up at the bus stop. Back at their house I had supper with Nina, Steinar, and Sondre's little brother, Henning. After playing video games in Henning's room, we sat in the living room to talk about the reason for my visit. Nina showed me albums and photos of Sondre. In the calendar on my phone I had a short description of him on his birthday, June 16. He had just turned seventeen when he was killed. Since we were both ardent Liverpool soccer club supporters, I felt that we had an extra bond. At his funeral, a Liverpool kit was draped over his coffin. "You'll never walk alone."

I watched a video of him and the rest of his friends singing the soccer anthem "Alt for Norge" (All for Norway) inside the Cafeteria on July 21, 2011. The next clip Nina showed me was from a festival in Orkdal on Saturday June 30, 2012, at a memorial service for Sondre. At the end of the service Nina, Henning, and ten members of the AUF sang "Alt for Norge" together.

"It was meant to be a real celebration of Sondre," she explained. "With music, loads of people, joy, and enthusiasm. And it was! I spent the whole evening in the festival tent serving beer."

"It might be fine to pull down the Cafeteria in a while, but at the moment it still feels so damn scary. It feels like Sondre might disappear from me when the building is demolished. I know it's stupid to think like that, but that's how it is. It just tears me apart inside thinking it could happen, that he could disappear not just physically but from my heart. Even though I know it's just nonsense, it's been so hard all the same. That's why the plans for Hegnhuset are so good, for me personally as well."

Just as I had explained the concept of Hegnhuset in detail to Signe Marie and Jørn a couple of weeks earlier, I also took my time going through it with Nina. The response was the same.

"We thought more of the building would be preserved. We need to keep the atmosphere of the inner room, to feel that the small hall is still how it is today."

I took notes and suggested different ways to resolve this problem. They responded. We had a lot to talk about, and we hadn't even mentioned the memorial yet. The hours flew by. And so did the last bus to

Trondheim—without me on board. It had been a nice and useful visit. I gave Nina a big hug and said goodbye, then Steinar drove me all the way to Trondheim, late as it was.

I lay awake for hours that night wondering how to deal with this. Could we manage to retain more of the Cafeteria building, even though that would clash with Erlend's basic idea of having a "sacred" interior and less important exterior? We would hopefully get an answer a couple of weeks later in New York.

Our stay in New York began with a guided tour of the 9/11 Memorial and Museum given by Alice and her colleagues. Their mantra before the opening had been that they would leave no stone unturned to achieve a result they were happy with. This in itself was the right starting point for any subsequent work with Hegnhuset.

I started telling them about my recent visits to the families around the country, and the rather negative feedback I had gotten from many of the bereaved. The others were probably not expecting that we would have to return to our discussions of the concept. It was quite a setback.

But these guys were used to working with complex challenges. No one lost heart; on the contrary, the energy levels in the room rose considerably. We set to work again. Section by section, room by room. We could meet the needs of all those who had lost their loved ones inside the building by retaining all the inner walls. When you were inside the old Cafeteria, you would see it how it was on the afternoon of July 22, 2011.

So the body of the building itself would remain, but Erlend still wanted the external façade, the characteristic green paneling, to go. Several people insisted that it was the inside, not the outside, that was the essential part. The discussions progressed, and Erlend kept sketching. The first draft had allowed for one of the old rooms to be used for remembrance, where families and friends could leave behind mementos and commemorate each of the victims. This now had to go, since preserving the existing rooms was more important.

The 495 outer posts, one for each of the survivors of the terrorist attack, were placed such that they created a semitransparent shell. This external structure in no way attempted to conceal the stories from within Hegnhuset but instead enabled life to continue at the campground outside without having the tragic history of the Cafeteria looming over it.

The sixty-nine inner vertical columns reached skyward, supporting the new roof. The new body structure was rotated off axis with the old building inside and aligned with the other buildings that would be built on Utøya. This would represent and highlight a break with the past, a new slice of history, a new chapter on the island. In the area surrounding the Cafeteria, but still inside the new Hegnhuset, the floor was lowered.

The remainder of the Cafeteria was thus given a sort of elevated position, which in fact recalled what the perspective had always been like from the ground outside. The distance between the floor and the windows at the southern end was exactly the same as it had been in 2011. Many young people had jumped out of these windows to escape the shooting inside.

In an extension of the preserved sections, facing the campground, a new learning center would open. It was important that it faced the camping ground, where there is activity mainly in the summer. We also wanted to keep the old foundations that the Cafeteria rests on in order to create a learning space underneath the existing building.

After spending two days criticizing every aspect of the building, the concept had changed from a minimalistic preservation project to a far more complex construction. The basic idea behind Hegnhuset remained as before, but all these modifications would alter the building significantly.

On our last day we presented our new plans to the staff at the 9/11 Memorial and Museum. It was a large team, consisting of extremely competent and experienced coworkers with expertise in every single aspect of what we had been working on—from the process itself to architecture, exhibition design, and education. Somewhat surprisingly, we were also asked if some people from Columbia University and the Norwegian Consulate in New York could attend the presentation. They obviously had high expectations over there for our project on a small island in faraway Norway. One of the concluding comments stayed with me after our trip to New York:

"Few other places targeted by terrorists manage to preserve their traumatic history in a dignified way that allows for both the needs of the bereaved *and* new life, all in one small building. If this Hegnhuset turns out how you have described it here today, it will be one of the top places in the world for conveying history."

Utøya rises from the ashes

I stand at the highest point of Utøya, the center of the island, with Hegnhuset at one end, the campground below, and a new "square" to the north. This is the place where the physical rehabilitation and revitalization of Utøya began.

The first time I came here this was a large, neglected area containing just gravel, an outdated water filling station, a battered white metal frame belonging to a big marquee, and the remains of the old tent where they used to serve waffles. The entrance to the Cafeteria was at one end. Everywhere else there was dense forest—birch trees, pines, and some tatty-looking spruces. The past lay untouched. Silence and stagnation had taken over. Laughter from the kiosk queue was long gone. The huge trees were stooped, hanging heavily over the open space. The paint was peeling off, and weeds were sprouting up through the gravel. Even though it was just weeks since this was a summer paradise for the young, Utøya had suddenly become shabby, gray, and much, much older.

Standing here today, I see the same area full of activity and new buildings. New life.

Three and a half years after the terrorist attack, in the autumn and winter of 2014, the preparations for the physical rebuilding of the island got underway. Each part of the three-part solution—commemoration, learning, and engagement—had been attributed a building project: the Clearing

(Lysningen), Hegnhuset, and the conference center Torget. But this last word—engagement—involved far more than simply building the practical facilities. The whole infrastructure had to be upgraded, the outdoor areas improved. The overgrown woodland needed thinning out, and the older buildings, which hadn't been maintained for some years, needed renovating.

We were now going to erect new buildings, and central areas of the island would be altered dramatically. It was therefore especially important that we took care of the old buildings in the best possible way. Nothing epitomized the past more than the Main Building and the Storehouse in the old yard. The Storehouse had been closed for several years and was strictly speaking condemned. The municipality had approved an application to pull it down, but there was no question of that happening now.

We applied to a number of foundations for funds and eventually got enough contributions to be able to restore the Storehouse to its original standard. It was dismantled plank by plank, and reassembled plank by plank, using specialist knowledge and handpicked materials.

Someone whose efforts have contributed enormously to the rebuilding of Utøya is Svein Haraldsen. It was this dexterous seventy-two-year-old carpenter who spent the autumn going up and down ladders at the Storehouse. He has worked as a carpenter almost his whole life, but despite all these years working in construction he shows few signs of wear and tear. His hair has only just started to go gray, and he probably still wields his hammer as effortlessly as when he first started out in 1965. Undeterred by rain or snowstorms, Svein renovated the whole Storehouse. He's the kind of man you have to persuade to come inside to take a coffee break. But when he finally did so, it was good to have the company of this modest, knowledgeable, humorous man. His mild manner provided a sharp contrast to the constant hammering and deafening noise he made in the Storehouse.

It was now never quiet outside our office in the Main Building, next door to the Storehouse. The island's transformation from unnatural silence to sawing and the banging in of nails came as a relief. In the past three years a lot had happened to the plans for the new Utøya, a lot had happened to our process and how things were handled after the terror attack, a lot had happened internally to the AUF and the collaboration with the support group—but little had happened on the island itself.

Jon was there every day taking care of the most essential maintenance matters, but he couldn't cope with the backlog of repairs all by himself. Slowly but surely decay was setting in. It was therefore satisfying for both him and me to see the Storehouse restored to its former glory. It heralded a brighter future.

The AUF and the architects from Fantastic Norway wanted to create an integrated village concept in the center of Utøya. This was the main idea behind the first plans that were presented—a village with a square, small streets, and areas that gave the buildings a vibrant, unified look. When planning the new buildings, we stressed the need for simplicity, yet we also wanted them to appear attractive and inviting. The façades would be made of wood, concrete, and glass. What the redevelopment would cost had not been a major issue initially. As a result, we then had the unenviable task of having to make cuts. The buildings had to be reduced in terms of size, technical complexity, and cost. We finally decided on drawings that we felt reflected the practical functions the new Utøya would need and that were within our budget. We had less than 60 million kroner to spend on this. Keeping costs down thus became an important aspect of my job.

When winter came, we made plans with the men in charge of felling trees and operating the excavator. The support beams of the buildings were hoisted into position, one after the other. They were impressive, almost cathedral-like. The basic structure of the new complex was ready in just a few weeks. The new buildings were placed north of the Cafeteria in an area of dense forest.

However, here at the top of the island there is also a concrete example of our occasional failure to reconcile the old with the new. In the case of our new conference center, Torget, we have had to sacrifice something from the past in order to make room for the future. As well as the woods, an iconic little building used to stand here—an outside toilet, actually. The AUF, like much of the younger generation in Europe at the time, became more left wing in the early 1970s, and this led to an open flirtation with radical jargon and symbols. Utøya adopted several place names during this period that are still used today. Examples of this are Bolshevik Cove and Menshevik Cove, after the two factions involved in the Russian Revolution in the early 1900s. Now back to the outhouse. The Vietnam War strongly influenced Utøya at the beginning of the 1970s. Songs were sung about Ho Chi Minh, and Utøya was declared a NATO-free zone. At one point some AUF youths went and stole a sign from the NATO camp outside Oslo. The sign was hung in the forest at the top of the island, pointing in the direction of the outhouse nearby. The outhouse immediately became known as the NATO loo. With music playing inside, it was the most pleasant toilet on Utøya until sometime in the 2000s. Now that the new buildings were going to be erected on the site of the NATO loo, it had to be moved. When we tried to lift the humble structure, however, it simply collapsed. With Jens Stoltenberg as the secretary general of NATO and without a NATO loo on Utøya anymore, it's doubtful that the opposition to this defense organization will ever be as fierce here again. By way of consolation, we hung the sign up in a different tree in 2015, and it still points toward the toilets—although these are now indoors. So time will tell whether AUF members on Utøya will continue to "shit on NATO," as the '70s slogan put it.

While the building works were in progress, a huge amount was also done by volunteers. With the solidarity, engagement, and hard work these collective efforts entail, they are essential to Utøya's identity. There was an almost endless need for people to clear up, clean, paint, and chop wood. The forest had already grown very dense, and in some places it was almost impenetrable. Between 2011 and the summer of 2015, over three hundred people put in over eight thousand hours of their spare time to get Utøya ready for its new life. Even though the support we received was invaluable, we had to acknowledge that it wasn't all about the work. Actually, it was probably not the physical effect of the volunteers' efforts that was the most important thing. It was the sense of belonging, coping, and camaraderie experienced by new and old AUF members, July 22 survivors, the bereaved, people who simply felt affected by the attack, youngsters wanting to help other youngsters, and complete strangers with a heart of gold.

One of these combined efforts took place in April 2015. Lars Henrik Øberg, Johannes Giske, and Ronja Breisnes, along with lots of other AUF members, came along to help. All three of them survived the massacre on July 22, 2011. "For me it's important to go to a summer camp on Utøya again. To prove to yourself, above all, that you can live with it," Lars Henrik told me at the time. They had experienced unimaginable trauma. But now they were back here, helping out. To rebuild themselves, and to rebuild Utøya.

The memorial on the island: the Clearing

From the top of the island I stroll northward down the path to the glade in the woodland on the hill. Although it's only one hundred meters away, it often takes ten minutes to walk there. There are always some fallen branches to remove, and the view down to the old yard and the hillside in the sun usually deserves a picture. Where the path leading from the open landscape ends in forest at the top, harebells and lilies of the valley replace the wood anemones. The sun breaks through the branches of the trees and warms up the ground. The small flowers reach for the light. It's often impossible to walk past without lying down to take close-ups of these wonders of nature.

The sounds from the campground have gone; lapping waves and rustling leaves have taken their place. At the northern tip of Utøya, just before the Path of Love leads out to Bolshevik Cove, I reach the glade. It's situated right above the path, a few meters higher up. It is particularly beautiful here with all the pine cones, flowers, and birds. A place for reflection and contemplation. I go further into the woods. Every meter I walk, every direction I look in, the scenery changes slightly. The memorial is visible between the tall pine trees straight ahead. More of these magnificent pines surround me. I look up at their reddish-brown trunks; I look all the way up to the top, where the branches dance in the wind, and see blue sky above.

It's these trees that create the sacred atmosphere. And it's these trees that bear the heaviest responsibility here in the glade. Suspended from the tall pines, a metallic ring hovers one and a half meters above the ground. Absorbing and adopting the colors around it, the ring is an impressive sight. In the winter it has a distinctly white glow to it, while now in the spring it reflects the surrounding forest. The names and ages of those who were killed at Utøya on July 22 are inscribed in the steel.

The only project that has remained unchanged since the first plans were made public in 2011 and 2012 is the plan to have a memorial on the island. The grief of those worst affected will never disappear. But for many this inconsolable sorrow has gradually become infused with warm memories too. The memorial in the woods has hopefully contributed to this in some small way.

In the summer of 2013 we had just about started work on this project. While the national memorials at Sørbråten and in Oslo were to have a public function, we wanted the one on Utøya to be a more private place, mainly for the bereaved and survivors. We wrote a memo to the AUF executive board presenting our recommendations. We thought it was vital that the memorial should be open so that it could represent as many as possible of those directly affected and provide a space for individual experiences. A memorial designed for reflection.

We appointed a working group to be responsible for the memorial. In the spring of 2014 we posed two questions: Should the victims' names be part of the memorial? And where should it be located? We got a lot of feedback at meetings, on the phone, by text, and in other ways. Not surprisingly, there was strong support for having the names as an intrinsic part of the design. Several families suggested that the age of each victim should also be included.

There were two points in particular that kept coming up: Don't place the memorial where anyone was killed. Each murder scene had to remain private; we shouldn't make the different locations public property. Don't choose a site near where the terrorist was arrested, either.

In the notes I took after we inspected the site together it says:

> A nameless spot in the woods to the north of the new buildings. Universal access is possible, or a path up from the Barn so you don't have to go through the busiest areas of the island to reach the memorial. I expect this place will be used a lot. It gets the evening sun, potentially has a view

over to the national memorial, and a (partial) view of the campground. Existing vegetation consists mainly of pines and undergrowth and some of it should be cleared for the sake of the view and the light. The area is naturally open like a small amphitheater with a view (this could be improved and made more obvious).

First and foremost, the memorial would be a place that was open enough to embrace everyone's memories. The design itself was important, but the design could only do part of the job. It was the location of the memorial that was crucial for the role it would play. The place that was chosen was in a shielded yet very integrated part of the island, just a short distance from the hillside and Utøya's political hub. In all its apparent simplicity, this is a worthy and beautiful site. The choice of a good location was essential for our work going forward.

We invited four teams of architects and landscape architects to take part in a competition to design the memorial. At the beginning of August 2014, they each submitted their proposal. The memorial committee presented these proposals and discussed them at meetings of the support group all over Norway. We went to the cities Tromsø, Ålesund, Molde, Sarpsborg, Oslo, and Bergen—north and south, east and west. I visited family after family in their homes, taking copies of the drawings with me. The various proposals were discussed by the AUF's executive board as well.

We were also contacted by individuals whose views on the memorial were not welcome at all. People with links to the Far Right became fiercely involved in the campaign to conserve Utøya, and they wanted to stop a memorial being raised on the island too. The Norwegian Defense League and Stop Islamization of Norway were especially active. Most of them expressed their hatred of the Norwegian Labor Party and the Workers' Youth League. Some of them said straight out that it was a matter of finishing what the perpetrator had started—and shutting down Utøya as a recruitment channel for the labor movement. It was particularly painful to know that bereaved families and survivors who genuinely believed that conservation was the answer were now being used by people with almost the same mentality as the mass murderer. It was upsetting for many of them to suddenly find themselves in Facebook groups with the terrorist's supporters. Despite these unwanted responses, it was out of the question for us to close the online form that was used for giving feedback.

It was important to agree on a coherent concept for Hegnhuset before the memorial process was finalized because of the balance we wanted to strike at Utøya. The functions of these two projects were at times misunderstood and muddled, even by the bereaved families we were in touch with. Hegnhuset was not meant as a unifying memorial, and the memorial was not meant to also have an educational aspect. This had been a guiding principle since we wrote the memo for the memorial process back in 2013. However, we wouldn't know if this whole vision actually worked until we saw the final designs and details of the two projects.

After an open and inclusive process in which the vast majority of the feedback came from those directly affected by July 22, we were ready to proceed with one of the memorial projects on November 28, 2014. With almost six hundred different responses, it was not an easy choice. We gathered the memorial committee at Youngstorget and went over all the proposals. I presented the views that had been expressed online, in emails, and in conversations with a large number of the bereaved families. In the end we chose the project designed by 3RW architects. The name of the memorial was *Lysningen*: the Clearing.

The small area in the north of the island where we find the Clearing is like a miniature Utøya. It has never been used very much and didn't play an important role on July 22, 2011. In many ways the spot has been an empty space, without any particular history attached to it. Yet it is anything but empty. The area is full of flowers, pine cones, bushes, trees, woodpeckers—and now butterflies.

When big trees fall down in the woods, the resulting organic process creates a glade or clearing—an open space where the sunlight reaches the forest floor, producing a rich diversity of nature.

When the architects began to create the memorial, they found something that would tie all the elements together: a butterfly. The mourning cloak is a large butterfly whose name retains the same reference to grief in other languages too, such as Norwegian (*sørgekåpe*), Swedish (*sorgmantel*), and German (*Traumermantel*). Its wings are dark with light edges, reminiscent of traditional mourning dress. The mourning cloak—known as the Camberwell beauty in Britain—is found along the Tyrifjord and on Utøya. It lays its eggs on birches and aspens, and when the adult butterfly emerges in the late spring it flies to the specific plants that it feeds on: ox-eye daisies, poppies, lilacs, and wild strawberries.

The architects behind the Clearing worked closely with an ecologist in order to examine the relationship between the host plants and food plants for the various butterflies on the island. They devised a map of Utøya showing which plants, flowers, and herbs these butterflies preferred to feed from when they emerged from the chrysalis in the spring. Just as architects normally design places using wood and stone, the memorial was now designed according to organic processes, sunlight conditions, soil, and plants. The circulation of butterflies between the many different places on the island and the memorial site was given a free rein.

The architects obviously realized that it would be challenging to suspend a ton of steel from the pine trees on Utøya. After all, it wasn't just going to hang there for a few months but for many, many years to come. They contacted a number of different people who make a living out of hanging things from trees. In late spring they came to inspect the site with a slightly eccentric Englishman, a tree surgeon called Glen Read. Glen had fifty years of experience working with trees. Jon soon dubbed him Dr. Tree. Glen carefully scraped the ground around the pines with his small tools, concluding that the trees were healthy and could certainly be used. But that wasn't all. In an inspiring little lecture in the woods, he told us how the trees that would bear the weight of the ring have roots covering the whole area; he told us about organic processes, the soil water, ground pressure, and the life cycle of trees. He said that no machines should be allowed into the area as their weight could damage the roots. There should be no digging where the roots were more than two centimeters in diameter, and none of the usual filling with layers separated by a geotextile as that would restrict the roots' oxygen uptake.

Next we began clearing the area where the memorial would be located. Volunteers and AUF members from all over the country joined in. Deciding which trees and bushes to remove was an important aspect of the preparations and collective efforts. The memorial had to adapt to the life of the forest without being marred by its constant changes. We cleared undergrowth and removed twigs, thorns, and scrub.

I sit down on the slate paving and look in at the circle. Parts of the terrain have been lowered to create a ledge where you can sit facing the center of the clearing. On the other side of the circle it has been raised, so you can sit looking out across the Tyrifjord and enjoy the beautiful sunset in the evening. Humans have gathered in circles throughout history—around campfires, to sing or to reflect. The circle is a particularly social form in natural surroundings, but it's also a symbol of camaraderie, belonging, and solidarity. I sit here today in an uplifting and sacred space in the woods. By removing spruces and deciduous trees from the memorial site, we acquired a natural clearing surrounded by dense vegetation. The light penetrates the forest, and the heat from the sun brings life to the plants in the ground that was previously so dark. Thanks to our skilled architects and biologists, it will remain light and open here without needing too much upkeep.

I walk around the ring, giving the metal a slight polish. When the sun shines, the names punched out of the steel cast light and shadows on the ground. As it moves across the sky, the sun shines through every single name in the course of a day. I walk around the outside of the ring reading the names inscribed there: Rune, Tamta, Carina, Ismail, Eivind, Tore, Margrethe, Guro, Steinar, Victoria, Åsta Sofie, Silje Merete, Gunnar. The order and significance of where the victims' names were placed was a particular concern during our work with the memorial since this was important for many of the bereaved. If we had chosen a plaque or some other kind of flat surface with names on it, like traditional memorials often have, it would be natural to start reading from the top left-hand corner and finish at the bottom right. Someone would then come first and someone last. On our ring of names there is no beginning and no end.

When we sent the ring to be made that summer, it was with just sixty of the sixty-nine names. It was disappointing that not all the names were included, but this was also to be expected. Alice Greenwald had given us a sound piece of advice when we discussed the memorial. In processes requiring the bereaved to give permission to use names, not everyone usually wants to participate in the beginning. Some people need more time than others. It was therefore essential that more names could be added later on. To ensure that all the parents would receive the letter requesting their permission, it was sent by registered mail. Everyone received a text message as well. When the deadline for replies expired, Alice's prediction proved correct. We didn't exert any unnecessary pressure to include the last names; they would appear when the families were ready.

It would soon be July 22 again. Work on the memorial entered its final phase. The ring was about to be produced, the area was being developed with paving slabs and ledges to sit on, and plants needed planting. Now that the process was coming to an end, we wondered if we could do something to enable the bereaved to participate physically, in addition to voicing their opinions and being heard. It's often important to use your body, to do something with your hands, when working through grief. So we invited everyone interested to come and help out at the memorial site one weekend in June, a few weeks before it was supposed to be finished. This time the invitation caused no misunderstandings, unlike a couple of years earlier. The response was overwhelming. A number of bereaved families, a lot of survivors, Utøya veterans, and others all joined in. My one-year-old daughter Aurora was there too.

We laid slate paving in the glade to make access easier for everyone. Kolbein, Viggo, Trond, and Bjarte led by example, all fine strapping men and bereaved fathers. Mani, Roy, Monica, Jon-Inge, and Linda put down soil and planted the carefully chosen plants. Gunhild and Lisbeth pushed the wheelbarrow up and down and made a new wood chip path through the forest. With everyone's combined efforts we created the place together.

The four parts comprising the ring of names were delivered a couple of days later. We had to carry them, lift them up, and assemble them—all by hand. No heavy machinery was allowed into the area; arborist Glen Read had been clear about that. Each section weighed 250 kilos, so it was quite a slog. As on so many other occasions in the task of rebuilding Utøya, people were happy to help when asked. This time it was an *Aftenposten* photographer who had to swap his camera for work gloves and aesthetics for muscle power. Five men, a few hours' work, and the ring was finally in place. One week before the July 22 anniversary, the Clearing—Utøya's memorial—was ready.

The following day an art critic came for a visit. I was rather skeptical about an art critic coming to see the Clearing. Our objective wasn't to create art, it wasn't meant for public consumption, and it wasn't a traditional memorial. It was a memorial *site*, a place for those directly affected. So I was greatly relieved to later read that the critic had understood what we were trying to achieve. In the national newspaper *VG* on July 14, 2015, it said:

> The memorial on Utøya works so well because it is not an artwork with a
> dominating design. Instead, it is an open solution that leaves individuals

to create their own story. As a result, it is a place that allows for future opportunities while also honoring the memory of those who were murdered. Both brutal and conciliatory at the same time. Overshadowed by the controversy around the national memorial, the AUF have quietly striven to create their own memorial on Utøya. It has turned out very well indeed.

It wasn't long before beautiful butterflies were flying northward to the memorial from all parts of the island. In their wake came some considerably larger creatures. From north and south, east and west. From Norway and abroad. People who were affected by July 22, the old and the young, teenagers and adults. Life was on its way back to Utøya, and there would always be room for the memories.

For the first time since the attacks, there was a memorial to go to. A memorial for the bereaved, by the bereaved.

When the day was over and everyone else had left by boat, there was just me left. As in previous years, I walked around the island one last time, just to check there was no danger of fire from burning candles and that all the doors were locked. The last thing I did was go back to the Clearing. It was so beautiful to see the place filled with love. Flowers hung from all the names, and the ground was covered in red roses.

There have been many fine gatherings at the Clearing on subsequent July 22 anniversaries. Nevertheless, it is all the other days of the year that the place is really meant for. Days like today. The slate flagstones I am sitting on are nice and warm, as the stone retains the heat from the sun throughout the day. This is important not just to make the place as comfortable as possible but also to attract the butterflies that seek out warm areas like this. I leave my seat on the ledge and walk the few meters around the ring over to the edge overlooking the Path of Love. The forest floor here is covered in slate slabs, carefully laid by Asgeir, Kolbein, Bjarte, Viggo, and Trond that weekend in June 2015. The slate paving makes access easier for people in wheelchairs, with prams, or who have difficulty walking, but it also prevents the ground from becoming overgrown. In addition, the paving stones are like a kind of arena where the cycles of nature are displayed. In the surrounding woods, pine cones, needles, and leaves disappear into the bushes and grass, yet here they are more in evidence. Each season has its characteristics, and there is comfort and beauty in all of them. Therefore, all the visible evidence of these cycles and the activities that go with them—raking leaves or tending plants—are important aspects of this memorial site.

Between the trees I look out over the Tyrifjord, toward the mountain range Norefjell and the sunset. The Path of Love winds its way along the water's edge, and I can hear the waves hitting the sloping rocks below. In a spot full of tall trees I can hear a woodpecker. When I walk, pine cones crunch underfoot. A butterfly flies off from the wildflowers in the glade. With its colorful wings it flutters up from the grass and settles on the ring. The light shines through the names, making them all visually unique. The shadows cast by the tall pines sweep across the Clearing, changing its appearance from hour to hour. Slices of light, sunshine, sky, plants, and trees.

The fact that the memorial is situated in an area where no one was killed on July 22, 2011, prompts feelings that aren't associated with trauma and tragedy but with reflection, memories, and stories about those whose lives were stolen from us. Although the place is not particularly big, it works just as well for the individuals who come to visit as for the groups we now regularly host. Whether it's their first time on Utøya or whether they are personally affected by July 22 and have been here before, there is room for different interpretations of grief at this memorial site, not just one or two. The design is fundamentally antiauthoritarian; it is both sophisticated and unpretentious at the same time. Whatever your social, cultural, or religious background, you should feel welcome here.

I bend down and enter the metal ring. It encircles me, the sound changes, the names are inverted and merge into one, like the multitude they represent; it's no longer the individual names themselves that matter to the same extent. Up against the sky, the ring frames the glade and the huge crowns of the trees supporting its weight. The ring moves in time with the trees. Because it's so heavy, it sways very slowly from side to side in the wind.

With a cloth in one hand I go out again and walk around the ring. I polish each of the names. It's exactly how we hoped the memorial would be. Something you could walk around and experience, interact with—not just look at. As I go round, I whisper a few words about each of the victims. Words that have been in my calendar for several years now. Words about people I have never met, but whose memory I am partially responsible for keeping alive.

Leila spread laughter and joy every single day. She was known for championing justice, solidarity, and democracy.

Steinar couldn't bear to see anyone left out and on their own.

Despite his short life, Gunnar's dreams of a better world with more openness and more justice will live on.

Music was a big part of Håkon's life, whether it was listening to music on his MP3 player, playing the tuba in the school band or the bass in his own band. His dreams were taken from him, but our memories of Håkon will always be with us and inspire us.

Monica wanted to train to be a doctor. Her dream was to work for Médecins Sans Frontières.

The national memorial

From the Clearing I can see across to a wooded headland one and a half kilometers further north. Here the national memorial Memory Wound, designed by the Swedish artist Jonas Dahlberg, should have been built years ago.

It was supposed to be a memorial for the nation of Norway. Memory Wound would consist of a forty meter long and three meter deep channel cut though the headland, a "wound" that was meant to dramatize the loss, with the names of the victims engraved in marble on the rock face.

There has long been a huge misunderstanding among the general public, including those affected by July 22 and the journalists who covered the story, that this memorial would be situated on Utøya itself. The fact is that it was planned for Sørbråten, a small promontory on the mainland about one and half kilometers north of the Utøya quay (Utøyakaien).

The processes and discussions concerning Utøya's future and whether people were for or against the national memorial at Sørbråten created at times a painful division among those affected by July 22. Many of those opposed to the AUF returning to Utøya also opposed the memorial at Sørbråten, and vice versa. Of course the situation wasn't quite so clear cut, but people's opinions on these two matters often coincided.

Whereas we gradually managed to work ourselves out of a downward spiral on Utøya, the suffering caused by the national memorial debate became worse and worse—for both the bereaved and the local residents.

When the government tried to improve the poor dialogue with the local community about the memorial at Sørbråten, wanting to engage in conversations with all the neighbors, the government officials arrived at their meetings with a lawyer. It is no understatement to say that the presence of a lawyer doesn't exactly invite trust and understanding.

The major challenges surrounding the national memorial have not just been a result of bad management on the part of the government. It has been upsetting to witness the level that the discussions have sunk to, especially locally. The media have given the impression that the entire local population was violently opposed to the memorial. The situation was far from black and white, however, and I think the media knew that too. But conflict sells.

"This memorial isn't for us. We don't need a memorial to remind us of what happened. We don't actually want a memorial here at all. What we would like, though, is a place we could go to in order to *forget* the attack. A place like that would be used a lot."

These words could have been uttered by many of our neighbors living along Utstranda, but they weren't. They were spoken by someone living near Ground Zero, in lower Manhattan, New York. It's perfectly understandable that local residents can have such views, and I respect them.

There are hundreds of nice people living in the Utstranda area. The actions of many of them on July 22, 2011, made a massive difference. However, a small group of opponents of the memorial have stirred up the conflict. They have made life difficult for those who have put forward good, fair arguments when discussing the memorial. Neighbors who have been positive toward the proposed memorial along Utstranda have been harassed and ostracized by the local community. Locals who had previously cleared the snow from their drives have refused to do so anymore. As a punishment, they have been deprived of boat berths that they have rented for over fifty years. The local paper has cast aspersions on their motives, and slander has reached new heights on several occasions. If you are in favor of a memorial and yet weren't awarded the Order of Merit by King Harald for your services on July 22, 2011, people say that you support it simply to ease your own conscience.

What this active little group actually stands for is the least mentioned aspect of the discussions about the national memorials. It's hard to understand why neither the media nor researchers have bothered to examine the views of these prime movers in the opposition to the memorial site. The group thrives on a hotchpotch of conspiracy theories about the memorial processes. It doesn't help to point out to them that the government responsible has consisted of the Conservative Party and the Progress Party because in their eyes, it's still the Labor Party that is behind everything. Just as they believe that the Labor Party is responsible for all the other negative things in Norway, not least immigration. They hate everything the Labor Party stands for and therefore can't bear the activity we have on Utøya. They regularly complain about it. They complain to Hole municipality, the Norwegian Public Roads Administration, and other government agencies; they complain to whomever it's possible to complain to. They do all they can to close down the island and stop our activities there.

It took a while for me to realize how deep-rooted this is, why they were so obsessed with putting every imaginable obstacle in our way. At one of the meetings we had with them, however, a presentation I gave to the local community, the views of some of the group members became clear:

"If only Breivik had done an even better job—then he would have made sure that fucking island was shut down for good."

Hate lives on, even among some of our closest neighbors.

In the winter of 2018, the AUF and the support group recommended dropping the whole Sørbråten project. We suggested to the government and the cabinet minister involved, Jan Tore Sanner, that the Utøya quay could be used instead. As it seemed to be the simplest—and perhaps only—solution, the governed agreed. Memorials are all the more powerful when they commemorate what happened where it happened. And Sørbråten had absolutely nothing to do with July 22. By transferring the memorial site from Sørbråten to the Utøya quay, we would remove the focus on July 22 from the local community and place it somewhere where there was already a connection with July 22. This coincided with the wishes of very many of the local residents.

The Utøya quay on the mainland was central when terror struck Norway on July 22, 2011. This was where the campers and guests came to take the boat to the island. This is also where the terrorist came, dressed as a policeman. Later that day, the quay became the base for one of the largest rescue operations to ever take place on Norwegian soil. This is where frozen, terrified teenagers came who had swum from the island or been picked up by brave locals in their boats. The Utøya quay was thus the focal point where events went from bad to worse. Yet it also represents rescue and survival.

A national memorial by the Utøya quay will seem meaningful by virtue of its history. It will highlight the connection between the events of July 22, 2011, in Oslo and on Utøya and become an integrated part of the whole concept involving memory and learning. A memorial site here will be the last link in the chain comprising the July 22 Center, the memorial planned for the new government building complex, Hegnhuset, and the Clearing. Its location is also in line with international practice, where memorials are placed at sites that are directly connected to the event. It is in line, not least, with our own experience. Where it happened.

Statsbygg (the Norwegian government's building commissioner and property developer) and their architects did a good job of winning local support and ensuring that the project respected our neighbors' wishes and needs. Yet in the autumn of 2020 the memorial dispute ended up in court all the same. The fact that it took a lawsuit for the matter to be settled gives a clear picture of how bad the government, municipal, and local processes had been.

Creating a national memorial is no easy task, but the whole process has suffered from the political leadership's poor awareness when it comes to memory politics. Selecting which parts of the past to memorialize in the present day doesn't happen by chance, nor is it a question of how the past really was. It's a question of building a shared identity. This is a process of great value to society. Comprehending the complexity and acknowledging the value of engaging in the conversation about commemorative sites has not been a priority in the national memorial process after July 22. This, combined with the lack of effort and understanding and the evasive attitude of politicians, has created a deplorable situation.

The editor in chief of the paper *Nationen* wrote in 2017 that "the government could do with a 'peacemaker' to deal with this matter, like the AUF have found in their new CEO on Utøya." These are kind words for us on Utøya, but above all they highlight something important that has been missing from the government's handling of the memorial process: clear leadership and the goal that the local community be able to lead more normal lives, too. With bureaucratic tunnel vision, the government has single-mindedly focused on establishing a memorial, not on helping the local residents to move on. They haven't been concerned with the big picture, or the process, just the narrow objective of the memorial itself.

The municipality of Hole itself has been terrified, not daring to deal with anything related to July 22, least of all a memorial. It has done what needs to be done but has avoided adopting an active role. The Utstranda residents' association has been taken over by a bunch of people whose hatred of government authorities knows no bounds. No one has concentrated on the most important thing: how to create a balanced, meaningful future, with the memorial as part of the overall vision. Without sound foundations, without a good process, it's hard to see how it is possible to create a powerful and important memorial site.

"The AUF have reclaimed Utøya. We want to reclaim our home, Utstranda, the way it used to be." Many people referred to this quotation during the lawsuit of autumn 2020. It's understandable to want life to return to how it was before. This applies in most situations; people long for the way things were before the problems started. The trouble is that it just isn't possible. Life will never go back to normal. It took some years before we managed to establish this as a basic approach to the work we do. Our discussions went nowhere until most people realized that we needed to create a new future, not just expect the old days to come back. If the rehabilitation of a community exposed to a terrorist attack overlooks or seeks to minimize the traumatic history, it will fail. It is not correct when some people say that the AUF has got its old Utøya back. But although the old Utøya no longer exists, there is now a new Utøya, where the past lives side by side with the present and the future, where memories live side by side with smiles, joy, and new life. This is something that some local residents have never wanted to acknowledge. Nor have the authorities ever attempted to see things in this way.

The national memorial at the Utøya quay opened in the spring of 2022. It is a place that represents loss and grief, but also rescue, bravery, and vitality. Like at Utøya itself, the memorial does not stand alone on the quay but is part of an active waterfront in an otherwise quiet neighborhood. The memorial therefore functions as both a transport hub in a thriving local community, whose most important task is to prepare for future generations of residents and guests, and a place that handles its traumatic history with dignity. A dynamic balance between memory and history on the one hand and renewal and new life on the other.

No Man Is an Island   131

Most, but not all, of our neighbors are happy with this, but as a society we have a responsibility to create arenas for remembrance—something I am sure has been achieved at the memorial on the quay. As most experts in this field emphasize, it is hard to see that the memorial itself can be a stronger reminder of the events of July 22 than Utøya is already—a view confirmed by the judgment passed by the Borgarting Court of Appeal. And the island exists as a constant reminder that neighbors can see from their properties on a daily basis.

If we have learned anything from Utøya, it's that an awareness of the function of memorials also requires an awareness of the processes, the stages of memory. It demands more than decisions taken solely for the sake of efficiency and results. When we are finally able one day to distance ourselves from the traumas of July 22, the dispute over the location of the national memorial will have unfortunately left a stain on Norway's reputation for the way we handled the aftermath of the attack.

The importance of the national support group

The path continues past the Clearing down to the Path of Love. To the left this takes us almost along the water's edge to the Pump House. To the right, down quite a steep cliff, is Bolshevik Cove. This is where the Path of Love ends, or begins. With the rocky Stoltenberget headland on one side, the Path of Love up the hill, and the so-called Utøya stadium (the soccer pitch) behind me, I go down to the cove. This has traditionally been associated with campfires, barbecues, guitar playing, swimming, private concerts, cold toes, and international dance shows.

Even though the history of the AUF and Utøya are closely entwined, far more people than just the labor movement's "faithful" have a strong connection to the island. Important volunteer organizations have been founded here, environmental organizations have passed controversial, groundbreaking resolutions, and religious organizations have celebrated and practiced their faith. Guests from all over the world have visited the island, drawn inspiration, and shared experiences. Nordic scout camps have been arranged on Utøya, and children's theaters have been regular guests here. When the lake was totally still, people would make small lanterns to float in it. The candle flames would flicker for hours out on the water.

Bolshevik Cove is no longer the same today. During the period of building, barges used to dock here. We had to fill it with stone and make an improvised quay. There wasn't actually that much to do as the Norwegian

Civil Defense and Directorate for Civil Protection had already turned the bay into a harbor in August 2011 in order to facilitate visits from people affected by the terror attack. We have now removed most of the stone, but the new road remains.

I take a few steps along the water's edge, clamber over the boulders, and lean back against the rock face. There's a small picture placed in a crevice here. The passport photo is of Torjus Jakobsen Blattmann. Torjus was deputy leader of the AUF in the city of Kristiansand and was at Utøya for the second time. He was murdered here on the northern tip of the island along with seven others. It was Torjus's father, Trond, who marked the place where his son died with this picture. I have often stopped off at the cove to see if the photo is still there.

Trond has been one of the most important figures involved in our endeavor to return to Utøya. Many would recognize him as the face of the national support group after July 22. Straight after the terrorist attacks he acted as a spokesperson for those affected. He was leader of the support group from its foundation in the autumn of 2011 until spring 2015. During this period Trond's input regarding how Utøya should be managed was invaluable. We spent hours discussing the support group's role in Utøya's future. Trond has never made a secret of his own views: Utøya had to reopen, the AUF had to return. At the same time, he always spoke up for the support group's members. His efforts have helped lay the groundwork that ensures that Utøya evolves in the right direction. Trond always gave his honest opinion, whether it was his full support or constructive feedback.

Even with the most difficult matters, in conversations about grief and despair, Trond always managed to create a positive atmosphere with his hope and enthusiasm. His cheerful disposition, sense of humor, and ready smile meant that this was the man I called when I needed solutions, productive discussions, and also a good laugh. It must have been an enormous strain to be so directly concerned with the immediate aftermath of July 22, on behalf of the many hundreds who were personally affected. Trond often mentioned that it was a way for him to process the shock, loss, and feelings. It helped to get involved, think about something else, do something constructive for his own sake and for so many others. It was understandable that he chose to resign as leader in 2015. The support group is meant to be unaffiliated with any political organization, which Trond felt was incompatible with his growing involvement in the Labor Party in his hometown of Kristiansand.

It's not very far from the photo of Torjus round to Stoltenberget. Clutching at branches, I make my way carefully over the wet stones from Bolshevik Cove to the northernmost point of the island. While the cove was renamed Bolsjevika in the 1970s, having been called Åkervika for many years, the name Stoltenberget is far more recent. In order to honor Thorvald and Jens Stoltenberg, father and son, the AUF decided to call the headland after them in 2010. The purely positive connotations of this name on Utøya didn't last for very long though.

One of the five who were killed here on July 22 was Synne Røyneland. According to the eulogy read aloud at the trial, Synne was artistic and passionate about societal issues. In her blog she wrote about difficult topics—the body, self-image, the way women are treated—but also about the little things we can do for each other in day-to-day life. It was Synne's mother, Lisbeth Røyneland, who took over the leadership of the support group when Trond stepped down.

Replacing a towering figure like Trond was no easy task. Although we already knew Lisbeth, we were still anxious to see how it would go. There was no doubt that she backed our objectives for Utøya, however. Her opinion piece in *Aftenposten* on July 4, 2014, had been an important declaration of support at a turbulent time. Among other things she wrote, "The extreme right is on the rise in Europe, and Norway is no exception. This is something we must fight. Politically engaged youth must continue to stand up for the values that were attacked. . . . For me, restoring Utøya and its outdoor areas is a clear signal of how highly we regard freedom and democracy." Whereas Trond played a vital part in shaping Utøya's future, Lisbeth has meant an enormous amount to the other projects. Ever since our work on Utøya started to take form I have been invited to participate in other processes, usually in collaboration with Lisbeth. We worked closely on setting up the July 22 Center in Oslo, which opened in 2015, and more recently on the opening of a temporary July 22 Center and location of the permanent center as part of the new government quarter. We have also been concerned with the challenges that the government faced regarding the national memorial. Lisbeth has given so much of herself, and to a large

No Man Is an Island 135

extent it is thanks to her that the stories from July 22 will be showcased publicly in Norway in the years to come.

I follow the path back from Stoltenberget through a small copse of trees and head for the soccer pitch. Aerial photos of Utøya give the impression that there's dense vegetation here. With the exception of the soccer field and the campground, it looks as though the whole island is covered in thick green forest. In reality, however, because the trees are mostly pines, there is some distance between the trunks. The landscape is quite open and easy to navigate, even if many places have become overgrown. The sound of the waves fades behind me. The wood in front of me opens up, and I arrive at the soccer pitch. There are no matches on today, just a few boys performing tricks with the ball near one of the goals. I know exactly where to walk to avoid getting my feet wet. Traces of where the road went over the pitch in August 2011 to handle all the equipment, all the cars, all the people, are less and less visible as the years go by.

In the woods up by the Clearing the trees rustle, a couple of branches snap, and then our goats come running out. A couple of years ago we decided that we needed help to keep the forest under control, so we started a collaboration with Helge, the so-called goat king of Håøya, an island just outside Oslo. Every spring Helge brings a new lot of young goats to us on Utøya. It's like paradise for them here, with loads of fresh buds, bushes, and undergrowth to enjoy all day long. They drink fresh water from the Tyrifjord, and there are many smooth rocks where they can bask in the sun. The goats are also great for lightening the mood. With all the places and moments evoking painful feelings on the island, it's so nice to see the cute animals put a smile on people's faces when they come trotting along. As soon as the goats realize that it's me walking here, not our goatherd, they shoot off elsewhere. There's no food to be had from me today.

SUMMER

The AUF comes home

I was in my office in the Main Building on the morning of Thursday August 6, 2015. The Clearing had been inaugurated two weeks earlier, and we were in no doubt that we had put in place the first of the three pillars: Utøya, a place for commemoration. Now it was time for the next one: Utøya, a place for engagement. Hundreds of enthusiastic AUF members were about to go back to camp.

For the first time since 2011, a summer camp would be held on Utøya again. This was what the AUF had been working so hard to achieve these past four years. We were ready for the most important occasion in the history of Utøya.

For some time, it was by no means certain that the AUF would ever arrange a summer camp on Utøya again. They had been obliged to consider a number of dilemmas and difficult questions following July 22. How should they proceed to ensure that the organization would come back? Not just back to Utøya, but also back to all their other activities. How could they reconcile different conceptions of time? How could they also be mindful of those who weren't ready for camp to start again?

The AUF consisted of a range of people—survivors of the July 22 attacks, older members who had spent much of their youth on the island but who weren't there on that tragic day, plus many new members who had never been to a summer camp, let alone Utøya. This meant that there were several things to take into account. Some young people needed to overcome their fears and traumas, while others needed information and a sense of ownership. The AUF's strategy was to promote Utøya in as many forums as possible. Together we arranged open days on the island with old and new AUF members showing visitors around. The AUF members' magazine did a special feature on the summer camp, and central members of the organization traveled around explaining how the camp on the island works. We made Utøya gift vouchers that were used by local AUF branches all over the country—not because they would generate such a vast amount of money but because it was a simple way to anchor Utøya's role in the organization. The central office renovated the Schoolhouse; the collective spirit was revitalized. We documented and publicized each big and small step that the AUF took.

In the years following 2011, the AUF had arranged its annual summer camp elsewhere. In 2013 and 2014 it was held at Gulsrud, which is also on the Tyrifjord, a thirty-minute boat ride away. One day during the camp there in 2014 boats sailed back and forth between Gulsrud and Utøya so that several hundred AUF youngsters could visit the organization's own island, most of them for the first time. They were met and shown around by older AUF members, then they planted trees and flowers, ate waffles, and left messages on the Value Tree. There was a beautiful ceremony to remember those who are no longer with us, and sixty-nine heart-shaped balloons were released into the sky. In many ways the day gave a small hint of things to come, with the AUF needing to strike the right balance between Utøya's negative and positive history. Both tears and laughter came naturally that day. It was important for the new generation who would attend camps on Utøya in the near future to get to know the island, with all its stories and traditions. "We're at our cabin for now," said Eskil, "but next year we'll be home."

Now "next year" had arrived. The AUF was coming home again. Eskil was no longer leader of the Workers' Youth League. He had stepped down at the national congress in 2014 and was succeeded by Mani Hussaini. Mani himself was not at Utøya on the day of the massacre, but he had long experience from the island, lost many of his closest friends in the attack, and worked at the AUF office in the period afterward. The new secretary general, and the person responsible for the camp's practical arrangements, was now Ragnhild Kaski. Renate Tårnes was organizational leader. Both of them knew Utøya very well, both of them were here on July 22, 2011, but neither of them had any actual experience of running the camp.

The day before camp started we had planned an opening of the island for over two hundred people who had contributed to the rebuilding of Utøya. Our new conference center, although far from ready and as yet unused, had still been given a certificate of completion from the municipality. Norwegian and international journalists covered the event. Dozens of survivors from July 22 were going to attend their first summer camp since 2011.

"Everything MUST go according to plan," was the last thing the executive board of the AUF said to me before the summer.

"Of course," I answered, well aware that this was highly unlikely considering so much was new and there had been so little time for practical preparations.

Thousands of individuals, organizations, and companies had helped Utøya become a central arena for young people. Hundreds of children and teenagers had sold waffles, arranged concerts, and held bazaars. Many important contributions had made the new Utøya possible.

It was a proper summer's day, with sunshine, blue skies, and an island glimmering with hope. When the first buses and cars full of participants arrived, the sight was overwhelming. Survivors of the attack, fresh new AUF members, veterans wanting to return to camp, donors, and other supporters. There were probably over fifteen hundred people at Utøya on the afternoon of August 6, 2015.

It was no joke having to deal with brand-new buildings that were hardly finished as well as brand-new personnel and at the same time provide four thousand meals a day. It was something of a logistical nightmare to organize all the boat transport, catering, trash collection, and so on. For those few days I was in charge of a campground for the very first time. We pulled it off! And the food was good. Jon made sure that the practical side of things went smoothly, in close contact with the various teams of AUF assistants. For the first time in twenty-five years, Jon was at a summer camp on Utøya without Monica at his side. For Jon, and many others besides, this was Utøya functioning as normal. At the same time, of course, everything was different.

Over twelve hundred enthusiastic participants attended the AUF summer camp in early August 2015. This was twice as many as in 2011. Some of them had been at Utøya on July 22; others were here for the first time. Some had only just become teenagers; others were pushing thirty. Some had had a hard time making it to the island; others had managed to put the terror behind them. All of them were gathered on Utøya to uphold the values that were attacked on July 22.

Many of those who had run for their lives just four years earlier were now responsible for selling waffles and organizing sports tournaments and political workshops and so on. They demonstrated an almost unfathomable resilience, will power, and determination. They were back at camp not only for themselves but also for the rest of us, for Utøya itself. The terrorist had failed. The youth had been attacked, and it was the youth that now fought back and led the way—stronger than ever before.

The AUF was back home.

To the Youth (translated by Rod Sinclair in 2004)

> *Neat stacks of cannon shells*
> *Row upon row*
> *Death to the life you love*
> *All that you know*
>
> *War is contempt for life*
> *Peace is creation*
> *Death's march is halted*
> *By determination*

Most Norwegians would recognize the original words taken from the poem "Til ungdommen," written by Nordahl Grieg in 1936 in response to the Spanish Civil War. It was sung on many occasions in the aftermath of July 22, 2011.

Here on Utøya the poem has a long history. On Wednesday, July 20, 2011, at four-thirty it once again became relevant when a memorial plaque containing Nordahl Grieg's text was unveiled at the top of the island.

The memorial honors Martin Schei from Førde and three other AUF members who died fighting for the International Brigades against Franco, Hitler, and Mussolini during the Spanish Civil War, 1936–39. It is the first memorial ever raised on the island, exactly seventy-five years since the war broke out.

Acknowledging the links between today's challenges and past events, understanding the connections between good and evil, is nothing new for the AUF or for Utøya. One of the things Eskil said in his speech two days before the mass shooting was "you have to know the past to understand the present and shape the future."

The AUF posted a news item about the plaque entitled "In Memory of Those Who Fell" on the organization's website on Friday, July 22, 2011, at ten in the morning. Just hours after this was posted, dozens more young AUF members had tragically fallen, this time not in a distant war against General Franco's fascist *cruzada* but as victims of a personal crusade led by a Norwegian right-wing extremist on the AUF's own island.

I walk the short distance from the memorial to victims of fascism eighty-five years ago down to the Cafeteria, where victims were cruelly taken from us by that same hateful ideology in 2011. It isn't far between the layers of history on Utøya.

The day after the summer camp ended in 2015, I was standing on the same spot as I am today. The only call I got that day was from the man who had written the post for the AUF website back in 2011, then a member of the youth organization, now president of the board of Utøya: Jan Christian. He congratulated me on a well-run camp but shortly afterward, planning ahead already, he asked: "What about the funding for Hegnhuset, then? How shall we go about it?"

There was no doubt that we had reached important milestones now that the Clearing was in place and the AUF's camp had returned to Utøya. The sight of the abandoned Cafeteria building, however, was a powerful reminder that our work was not yet over.

We needed to build Hegnhuset.

If it was to be a reality, we needed more financial backing. We had already spent the funds earmarked for redeveloping Utøya on constructing Torget and restoring the older buildings and on infrastructure and the Clearing.

"Here we go again," smiled Jon.

Where could we find new funding—and the right kind of funding? It had been complicated working with Utøya after July 22, 2011. We had kept having to revise our plans and make minor or major alterations. Decisions were reached after a lengthy, detailed, and organic process, so we didn't want to apply for funds that would bind us to rigid time frames and a fixed direction. A lot of people assumed that the redevelopment was publicly financed, but it wasn't.

When we returned the gifts of money from municipalities and other public bodies after the rose processions in 2011, we also lost the chance to apply for public funding in the future. Or rather, we could of course have applied again, and this could well have been a potential source of financial support, but we had deliberately decided against it. This was also the case with Hegnhuset.

With the funding secured, we could have finished building in the summer of 2016. This was important not just for those directly affected by the attack but also for Utøya's identity and our activities on the island. Leaving the Cafeteria building bare and untouched was not a good solution, especially now that we had established a coherent concept. Yet we simply didn't have the money.

Although we hadn't previously been in touch with any private foundations, we now decided to contact Knut Olav Åmås at Fritt Ord, a Norwegian nonprofit foundation that promotes the freedom of expression. They were willing to contribute. So was the Savings Bank Foundation DNB, which generously gave us 3 million kroner. Jan Christian and I continued to work on the project. The budget was 15 million kroner—a considerable amount of money, yet a relatively small sum for such an important building for Norway and such an essential building for Utøya. Labour party leader Jonas Gahr Støre had been very supportive ever since we presented the concept to him. I think he immediately realized the value of it, with its implications extending far beyond the labor movement. Before long he told us that the Labor Party wished to help finance the building and that he was working closely with Gerd Kristiansen, leader of the Norwegian Confederation of Trade Unions, to obtain their support as well. At the party's national congress in the spring of 2015, Jonas and Gerd entered the stage to reveal that they had secured a total of 10 million kroner. A total of 13,5 million pledged so far. We were nearly there.

We managed to come up with the remainder ourselves. In addition to Utøya itself, the AUF owns some property on the mainland. Before the construction work could begin, the municipality had decided that the Norwegian Public Roads Administration needed to approve the ramp down from the county road to the quay. As a result, a new, upgraded ramp and car park had to be built. The remaining section of the plot, which was still unused, consisted of an old house and an outhouse situated on a steep slope, where the servants of the rich owners from the 1890s lived while they took care of the island for their masters. The situation was clear. If we divided off this part of the land and sold it, we could raise the sum that we needed. Our plans for Hegnhuset would finally be realized.

Hegnhuset is finally built

By the winter of 2015 almost everything was ready and the building works could begin. The first step was to remove the sections of the old Cafeteria that were not going to be preserved. The dining hall had already gone, so now it was the distinctive entrance with the kiosk and the main doors that had to be demolished first.

When the dining hall was removed in 2014, it mattered less in a way. This area was of little importance, both on July 22 itself and to the building's exterior appearance. The next step was entirely different. One of the best-known images from Utøya on July 22 is the photo taken from the entrance to the Cafeteria building, with the corridor full of shoes and boots that were left behind. This place would now disappear. Large sections of the corridor and kiosk and parts of the great hall and kitchen would also be demolished. Lost forever.

I had mixed feelings when the excavator arrived at Utøya that day. Were we 100 percent sure that this was the right thing to do? Was the construction of Hegnhuset the best way to manage the Cafeteria's history? Had we correctly defined how much of the old building we should keep? We had considered these questions countless times before. I had had a temporary wall erected in the great hall so we could more easily picture what this would do to the room. Several had been shot dead in the far corner of the great hall, making this an important area. Having moved the partition wall back and forth, we decided to cut off the great hall one meter further north, thus retaining more of it. Feeling our way like this often resulted in new drawings, yet this never seemed to bother Erlend. He realized that such details were crucial for the people who knew the old building well.

Before the jaws of the excavator removed the first part of the Cafeteria, I walked through the whole building for the very last time. If felt right on behalf of several generations to bid farewell to this place that so many had known. Here was the kiosk, where hundreds of thousands of waffles had been made and sold over the decades. This was where you went to satisfy your sugar cravings with sweets, cola, or a lollipop. Here was the kitchen, where thousands of youngsters had been served meatballs and potatoes, where many a future AUF leader had stood chopping onions until their tears ran dry. It was here that several hundred young people had crammed together to hear Gro Harlem Brundtland tell the captivated campers about her long life in politics.

The places where so many people had been scarred for life, where teenagers had died but also saved each other, these would largely remain. They would be preserved, and in many ways highlighted, inside the new Hegnhuset. The places that would be lost, on the other hand, had in many ways served a different purpose, having filled thousands of youngsters with joy, enthusiasm, chocolate, waffles, lollipops, and major political speeches. It took some time, this last stroll around the Cafeteria building.

The demolition lasted for some weeks; the Cafeteria was taken apart piece by piece. Then once this job was done, some quite extensive groundwork was required. Before we could start on this next phase of the construction works, however, we had to be certain that all the drawings were correct. Most importantly, the actual position of the building had to be precise—which it still wasn't.

Ever since deciding to retain parts of the Cafeteria building, we had also promised all the bereaved that nothing would be built where any of the victims were found. We knew that all the families had been given GPS coordinates by the police. We also knew that these didn't necessarily coincide with the precise places where the youngsters had died; some were moved by their friends in an attempt to save them. For many of the bereaved this position was still their own sacred site, the official place where their loved one was last alive.

The challenge for us was get an overview of all the positions around the island, and specifically the Cafeteria building. Most of the places were in areas where there wouldn't be any building works anyway, such as by the Path of Love, the pump house, Bolshevik Cove, Stoltenberget, and so on. But we knew that several had been killed in front of the old kiosk in the Cafeteria and by the steps on the south side. We were reluctant to ask each of the families to send us their GPS coordinates, so we needed to ask the police instead. Yet again, this was easier said than done.

For weeks I was passed from one person to the next at the National Police Directorate, the Ministry of Justice and Public Security, and the National Criminal Investigation Service. No one could, or would, give me this information. Finally I got hold of a map of the island showing the individual crime scenes, but no one could tell me if the dots on the map were accurate or if they had been used for illustration purposes. I had to know the exact locations, the actual spots. I didn't give up, and in the end I was sent an anonymized overview of the GPS coordinates for the crime scenes on the island. At last I had what I needed, and I forwarded it immediately to Erlend. His reply was disheartening. In order to keep my promises to the bereaved, we would have to move the whole building slightly northward. This would have major repercussions for how we could make use of the floor space in the various parts of Hegnhuset and for what we could keep of the old Cafeteria.

Back to the drawing board.

Now that we once again had to reconsider the floor areas, we saw that the number of square meters allocated for the forward-looking activity, for the democracy workshop, was considerably reduced. Just as we wanted the whole of Utøya to strike a dynamic balance between memories and new life, the past and present, serious reflection and engagement, we also hoped to achieve this balance inside Hegnhuset. By preserving the affected sections of the Cafeteria building as they were on the afternoon of July 22, 2011, and by telling the stories from that day via text messages and words spoken, we wanted to make time stand still here on the inside. The danger was that we would create a distance between the exterior and interior, a rupture between the new life on the outside and the painful darkness on the inside. Commemoration, learning, engagement. A whole concept. Without one of them, they would all collapse. Having to move the new protective structure around the Cafeteria upset this balance. The area devoted to the past took too much room.

Several times I found myself desperately arguing that it would be alright after all. But Jan Christian kept sending me Excel spreadsheets showing area calculations and percentages. Not a day passed without a new reason for us to make major changes. I was probably just exhausted, because deep down I knew that he was right. We had to do this properly.

The lower ground floor of Hegnhuset, the place designated for learning purposes, became crucial. We had intended to use this area for the democracy workshop and for relating the events of July 22. Now that there was less space, something had to be done. The answer was to move the July 22 timeline to the corridor of the old Cafeteria building. It was possible to do this without affecting the crime scenes or places displaying visible traces of the attack. By moving Hegnhuset itself slightly to the north, we also gained a few extra meters of the old corridor, making it better suited for bringing together accounts from the massacre. Above all, it gave us the advantage of being able to further exploit the area for conveying history. Raised up, inside the old building, would be the story of July 22, while the focus below would be on learning and the future. Separate, distinct, but still closely linked together.

Once again we had been right to take our time, leaving no stone unturned in our search for the best solutions. We had established the position of Hegnhuset and determined the floor space—this time the decisions were final. The groundwork could begin and Hegnhuset could be built.

For someone like me, with no experience of building works or architecture, the construction of the protective structure itself seemed like a gigantic Lego jigsaw puzzle. With a total area of 572 square meters and a roof supported by sixty-nine wooden pillars, the prefabricated elements needed to be carefully put in place. These columns had a physical dimension, and together they would stand like figures to create the inner space. Surrounding these on the outside, the 495 lower posts would safeguard the interior by representing the people who had survived the attack on Utøya.

Even though we had emphasized that these pillars, both the internal and external ones, would not correspond to precise individuals but simply symbolize all those directly affected, the work involved in erecting them still had a personal feel to it and required a lot of care. Without mentioning this to the people employed by our contractor Høyt og Lavt, we saw that they understood the situation and took their work very seriously.

The new roof, which would be supported by the sixty-nine columns, consisted of eight laminated wooden joists, each measuring twenty-four meters in length. It was a technically demanding project to put them in place. As soon as the building works got started back in the winter of 2014, we had used a barge attached to the bow of MS *Thorbjørn*. The barge had traveled countless times back and forth across the Tyrifjord carrying concrete, planks, workers, volunteers, glass, steel, and everything else needed to create new buildings and infrastructure. But now the barge couldn't help us anymore: the joists for Hegnhuset were too big. Instead, they were flown over by helicopter one by one, with the campground providing a perfectly soft landing.

In the space between the sixty-nine inner columns and the outer protective structure, there would be a walkway around the whole building, well shielded by the jutting-out roof. We would have five different entrances to the building from here, ensuring universal access to all parts of Hegnhuset. The walkway would be widened to allow freedom of movement and flow, preventing it from feeling enclosed. In order to achieve this, a great deal of cement work awaited us.

In the area south of and under the old Cafeteria building we intended to create a democracy workshop, a learning center where we hoped to have youth engaged in activities. It was now necessary to partially excavate the ground underneath the old Cafeteria in order to increase the available area somewhat. Doing this manually would have been far too demanding, but luckily there was just enough room for the smallest mini digger to fit below the building. We removed small amounts of rock and soil at a time, and in the end we obtained the floor space we wanted.

In the spring of 2016 the external protective shell was finished. These posts shield the interior in the preserved section of the Cafeteria and provide access to Hegnhuset through a charged spatial sequence. The safeguarding structure surrounds the whole building. Between each post you can see in from the outside and view the scenery from the inside. However, this protective shell also provides direction and restraint, clear entrances and exits where you feel caught in the building's symbolic components. Trapped but apparently free.

No Man Is an Island 151

Erlend thought it was important to create inequality between the pillars. They were not meant to be the same size or equally spaced. While the openings are constant, the ways in and out are not supposed to be obvious; they are placed at random. This solution was chosen in order to emphasize the role that chance played in the decisions made on that fatal day.

Unfiltered sources

The July 22 Center in the government quarter in Oslo presents the course of events by means of photos, texts, film, and artifacts. The exhibition also focuses on the immediate reactions, the many expressions of grief and solidarity in the days that followed, and the trial the year after. All the main texts used in the exhibition are taken from the verdict delivered in Oslo District Court on August 24, 2012. Everything used in the exhibition comes from the publicly available sources constituting Norway's narrative for that day. At Utøya, however, we are in a much more private place. It's not the nation's story we want to tell but the island's own story. If there was one place where it was possible to use unfiltered sources, the words of those who were there at the time, their private communication, we believed it was here on Utøya.

There were 564 people at Utøya on the afternoon of July 22, 2011. This day presented impossible choices for all of them. Was it best to run or hide, go right or left along the Path of Love, swim across the lake or stay on the island, try to find cover or keep moving, huddle together or spread out? After a while they could hear sirens from the mainland, and at one point also the whirring of a helicopter overhead. But where were the emergency services? Why did nobody come?

In situations like these you use what you have at hand—your phone. People used their phones to make calls but also to send texts. A lot of texts. Texts that could be sent from phones that were muted. Texts that were sent from an iPhone passed around inside a cramped toilet stall in the Cafeteria building. Texts that were sent from the Schoolhouse, where almost fifty youngsters had sought refuge with volunteers from Norwegian People's Aid. Texts sent by teenagers who were trying to keep moving away from the gunfire. Texts sent from hiding places around the island where young people lay, stood, or sat holding each other, comforting each other, and doing their best to protect each other. Hiding places that proved to be safe for some but not for others.

At this point we brought in architect Atle Aas to help us with Hegnhuset. He had already worked on a number of commemorative and educational projects previously and came to us straight from the July 22 Center, where he had been the architect in charge. It was Atle who suggested using text messages as a powerful storytelling technique. He soon convinced Tor Einar and myself, and we decided to structure the narrative about that day around such texts—as long as enough people wanted to share them with us, of course.

Whether it was a good idea to tell this story using text messages depended on those concerned also thinking it was a good idea. And we were completely dependent on them wanting to share their own texts with us. Even though by this stage we had a dialogue with most of the bereaved families and dozens of survivors, this wasn't something we wished to ask them about directly. The information was therefore spread by word of mouth and on social media, in newsletters and internally within the AUF and the support group. The response exceeded all our expectations. Most of the people who contacted us had texts to offer, yet many also got in touch to explain that they no longer had any. Several years had passed and old mobile phones get mislaid or thrown away. A lot of the phones that messages were sent from now lay at the bottom of the Tyrifjord; they were lost or broken. It was therefore often the parents, the recipients of the texts, who had kept the messages and who now chose to forward them to us.

The texts sent that Friday afternoon are sources that bring us as close as we can get to the most traumatic incident in Norwegian postwar history. They are unfiltered sources, words from those who were there. Every single text contains a much bigger story, a tragic memory for hundreds of young people. The last words some of them ever wrote.

Call the police, someone's shooting on the island. We've locked ourselves in the loo in the Cafeteria building. At least 100 injured.

Sorry for everything. Love you.

Mum, everything's not okay! We're being attacked with guns!!

What kind of guns?

Call the police! Ask them to come!

Hasn't anyone done that? Aren't there any adults there?

Yes! But Mum, I might get killed!!! Help us! It's an attack on the Labor Party!

I've talked to the police. Call me.

Call me.

I've talked to the police again. They'll be at the island any minute. Call me. Should I come?

Call me. Shall I come and get you?

Shall I come?

Please call me. I must know where you are, then I can come and get you.

Ingvild's OK. Shot in the leg but conscious and calm. We're waiting to be evacuated.

We placed the text messages on a timeline. A timeline where they can be read individually or as part of a collective narrative about those who were on Utøya, part of a context, where the messages are connected to the events around the island in the course of these hours, and to what was happening on the mainland and in Oslo.

Atle and Tor Einar sat glued to the screen for days shaping the narrative how we wanted to tell it. New input kept coming, suggestions for changes to be made here and there. We went from lots of pictures to a few, to none, to a selection. In the end it all came together, a moving account conveyed in a straightforward manner.

Directly to new generations from the people who were there at the time.

One of the most important new buildings in the world

When the summer came we started work on the last phase of Hegnhuset. New walls were erected in the subterranean democracy workshop. The walls down here were completely white, devoid of content. We discussed at length whether we should use this area for exhibitions, to tell different stories that would contribute to the work taking place here. Our conclusion was to leave the walls bare. It would be up to young people themselves, the coming generations, to use this space and take responsibility for the future of democracy. It was their thoughts, opinions, arguments, and counterarguments that would adorn these walls.

The sole exception was a poem that we felt worked well here. It is both painful and comforting, concise and to the point. The poem is called "etter 22. juli"—"after july 22"—and was written by Frode Grytten (translated by Robert Ferguson).

> after we were blown to pieces
> after friday fell apart in our hands
> after we had to learn norwegian all over again
> after the grief reached the roots of our hair
> after the days began raining down over us
>
> words survive a nine millimetre glock
> love is stronger than a five hundred kilo bomb
> holding hands is mightier than a loading motion

> a little kiss worth more than fifteen hundred pages of hate
> a we worth so much more than an i
>
> there'll be another july twenty two, there must be
> a ferry to carry other beating hearts across
> tents pitched on the green grass
> the kiss of the morning to awaken the island
> hey, hey, time to get up and change the world

All the new walls were placed at the same angle as the rest of Hegnhuset, an angle that highlights the distinction between what we added and what was already there. Once the timeline with the text messages from July 22 was finished, it was carefully mounted in the corridor of the old Cafeteria. Then we just needed to fix the lighting, sand the concrete floor, and clean up—and the building was ready.

A building that preserves the memory of the most brutal event in Norwegian postwar history.

The commemoration ceremony in 2016 was different; it was now five years since the attacks. The day was extra special for us since Hegnhuset was finally completed, and it was the first time that the vast majority of the bereaved, survivors, and others affected would see the result. How would they react?

I was nervous about how those who had a close connection to the old Cafeteria building—Nina, Freddy, Gunhild, Marit, Signe Marie, Jørn, Ole Martin, Ina, and the others—would react. It was even more stressful that day because the prime minister and the royal family came to visit as well, which meant a lot of security measures and a strict plan that we needed to follow. Of course these visits were great, but I have to admit that they weren't our top priority. This day was for the families. One after the other they arrived, and most of them also visited the new building. Although Hegnhuset was not the memorial site for everyone, it was the learning site to be shared by all, the place that told the stories from July 22.

I talked to hundreds of people that day and got a lot of hugs and positive comments. Something I will never forget, however, is when Freddy appeared from Hegnhuset and headed straight for me. Freddy and I have discussed a great deal, argued as well; we have been in strong disagreement but have always maintained a constructive dialogue. We have talked a lot about the Cafeteria building, where his daughter Elisabeth was murdered.

No Man Is an Island 157

In public and in the media, the tone hasn't always been that friendly. As he now came striding purposefully toward me, I was unsure what would happen. Would I get a punch in the stomach or a clap on the shoulder? The moment when Freddy gave me a massive hug will always stay with me.

"It's amazing that it worked, Jørgen. I must still get used it being so different on the outside, but I can still be with Elisabeth on the inside. Together we managed to do this."

How do you commemorate a life?

In 2016 we kept aside part of the democracy workshop in Hegnhuset facing the lake in the west for a project that we certainly wanted to include but that for various reasons didn't materialize until three years later. It would tell the stories of the people we had lost. In the presentations we made for the support group back in 2014, in our communications with the media, in the brochures we made to finance the building, it said: "By means of their photos, names, and stories, all the individuals will be remembered by everyone who comes here. Remembered for how they lived, not just how they died. Remembered as the individuals they were, not just as a number."

In the summer of 2019 the so-called Memory Book was finally ready. The book is suspended at eye level between the ceiling and the floor, like a beautiful installation. It is circular, without a beginning, end, or hard covers. Visitors can open it, then it closes itself afterward. It contains pictures and texts that tell you a bit about what the victims enjoyed doing, what they were like, what inspired them.

The book was made in close collaboration with the bereaved families, who provided both photos and texts. Before we created the Memory Book, the dead were missing. We had their names, we had the pillars of Hegnhuset, but no faces, no personalities. For this reason the Memory Book is one of our most important projects since the redevelopment was completed in 2016.

No Man Is an Island 159

Why did it take so long? The idea was conceived back in 2014. We have blamed the delay on the conflicts surrounding the national memorial in Hole, which have been so distressing for many of the parents. This is true, it was an important factor, but has it also been something of an excuse? This is a delicate, demanding matter. Have we postponed it in order to avoid doing the job we had to do?

Neither Utøya nor the July 22 Center in Oslo has focused solely on the victims of the terrorist attacks. Our work on Utøya hasn't been grounded in telling the stories of those we lost. There has of course been an important element of this, although we have never intended to be another July 22 Center, but nor has this center told the murder victims' stories in any depth.

In the intervening years a lot of emphasis has been placed on learning and how the July 22 Center can evolve going forward. A great deal of work has been done. However, until 2020 the commemorative focus of the July 22 Center in Oslo was unchanged: a memorial room consisting of a portrait of each of the dead. These portraits have been important for many reasons—they give an impression of the extent of the attacks, they give the victims an identity—yet I still sympathize with the views of the bereaved families who think that this hasn't been sufficient.

The lack of depth to this commemorative focus is not due to any ill will. I think it's due to the fact that this is an extremely difficult matter to deal with. It's easy to say that these stories should have been an essential element. But then what about the families who don't want their loved one's life exposed in a national center?

The challenges we have had with the Memory Book on Utøya clearly illustrate this. First of all, we needed the families to provide us with pictures and texts. To make this easier, we told the parents that they could use the eulogies read aloud at the trial to help them. These were the words I obtained from the National Archives of Norway some time ago and that I have had in my calendar to mark the birthdays of all those who died.

A large number of families couldn't face it; they couldn't or wouldn't expose themselves to more suffering by having to write that kind of tribute again. But there were others who modified the old one or else wrote a completely new text. Finding photos wasn't always easy either. Some parents have lots of pictures of their children, while others have few. It was challenging for many families that our project required several photos. For the families who didn't have a lot of good pictures of their dead son or daughter it was particularly hard. So many of the victims were in their teens, an age when posing for your parents is not especially popular. Several parents contacted me to say that they didn't have any photos other than childhood ones, so they didn't want to take part in the project.

A further complication was caused by the divided families. Some parents were divorced and didn't speak to each other. Others were married but had opposing views. Some thought that the Memory Book contained too much, others too little. In addition there were cultural differences among the many people concerned. It was all very delicate.

We had taken the initiative to do something for the parents that we simply thought would be beautiful and important but that actually sparked a process that also caused hostility, arguments, and ill feeling. Strong emotions must be respected, and thus it is important to proceed with humility.

We have grown to realize that you must commemorate life, not just death. The deceased deserve to be remembered for more than the place and the way they were murdered. Today the Memory Book contains the stories of fewer than fifty-five of those who died. Time will tell if the rest will one day join them. Whenever the families themselves are ready, so are we.

This is yet another example of how complex the process of rebuilding Utøya has been on so many levels. And if we are to learn from our experience, there is no point in painting a rosy picture of it. The decision to demolish the Cafeteria building upset many people and was a divisive factor for a long time. The decision that the AUF would return to the island was the right one, and it had already been taken before I came on board in August 2011. Yet this too caused a lot of people pain.

It's natural to wonder why so many of those affected by July 22 have taken longer to return to normal life than the specialists expected. Part of the explanation might be that they have suffered a devastating experience that received a lot of media coverage and they have been retraumatized by events over time. It is also reasonable to assume that some of the bereaved have experienced strong reactions later than others, partly because their private mourning was displaced by everything else they had to deal with.

I have often wondered how much of this is due to the process that we have been responsible for. Should we have done things differently?

Undoubtedly. When a grieving mother calls me the reincarnation of Breivik, it's obvious that not everything has gone as it should.

We could have done with more help to get in touch with the families. We could have spent more time with them, had more in-depth discussions. I keep thinking that I should have had more conversations with the bereaved, more visits, more meetings with the survivors. And it's highly likely that all this would have led to a better process, a better result, and helped the many people concerned on an emotional level.

As one of the fathers said to me: "All the extra strain caused by your plans means that I don't get the peace of mind to process the grief properly. It's a distraction that keeps ripping the scab off this wound so it just keeps bleeding."

It's still hard to accept that since taking charge once the plans were presented, I have imposed an additional burden on these people who had already suffered so much.

Even though we must acknowledge the negative impact of the process we have implemented, experts stress that we should in no way blame it entirely. What is unique about July 22 compared with other traumatic incidents is that it involved the massacre of so many young teenagers. The brutality was unprecedented, the trauma was massive. Furthermore, much of the data indicate that far from all the bereaved have received sufficient or specialized grief and trauma therapy. It also appears that in some cases the families' support apparatus and social network have stopped providing help too early on, since it is difficult to understand the long-term effects of traumatic grief.

On the other hand, the progress we have made on Utøya—with the process, conversations, and the way we now commemorate their loved ones—is one of the most positive elements in the post–July 22 period for many of those affected.

Building a workshop for democracy

Since its opening in 2016, it has been our prime concern to fill Hegnhuset with activity. This also meant a definite shift in how we worked and what we did. Having basically handled and led a process, a sort of combined vision and peace process where we were constantly seeking answers and solutions, we were now more sure about what we wanted to do and how we could achieve it.

In developing Utøya as a learning center, a place for promoting democracy, for combatting radicalization and extremism, it was natural to focus on right-wing extremism. Ever since Martin Schei went off to Spain to fight the fascists in 1937, straight from Utøya, the island's history has been about exactly that: standing up to right-wing extremism and fascism. Breivik may have been a lone wolf and a loser, but he wasn't alone in having such a hateful ideology. He didn't come from nowhere; he hadn't created his own world. In the baggage he had with him on Utøya there weren't just weapons and ammunition; there were also ideas convincing him he was doing the right thing. The attacks of July 22 would not have happened without being anchored in something. And the hate so brutally manifested by the terrorist lives on in a number of circles.

You might have thought that these circles would have gone quiet after July 22. Unfortunately, however, a large number of AUF members and survivors of the attack on Utøya can confirm that this isn't the case. There are so many examples of such hatred. Eskil Pedersen had already started receiving messages on July 23, the day after the massacre.

"It's not over. Call the hospital. God save the King."

A lot of people found that all the death threats and hate calmed down for a while, only to start again later. At times it has exploded. For others, harassment and threats have been the norm ever since 2011.

> "Hope to see you buried at Utøya next year :) You fucking coward. Pity Breivik didn't kill you, otherwise he did a pretty good job."

> "Sorry to say it, but you're living on borrowed time. Just wait till next year's AUF camp. If you thought 2011 was a massacre, you'd better not go next year. . . . It'll also be the last year a Stoltenberg will enjoy the Norwegian limelight, oddly enough."

> "Anders Behring Breivik did a fantastic job. Well done. What would we do without him. Hope he repeats this success, then we'll be rid of all those asylum seeker groupies on Utøya."

One cold spring day during the construction of Hegnhuset, I came to work on Utøya as usual. Fredrik, the contractor's supervisor, asked me to come down to the building site. I walked over to the campground, past the fences, across the still damp, freshly laid concrete floor and came to a stop under the old Cafeteria. During the weekend, someone had broken into the area and made their way down here, Fredrik informed me. Here in the dark, someone had scratched a large swastika into the subterranean floor.

Unlike the tagging of the pump house some years earlier, this was not done by a well-intentioned idiot. The terrorist's ideology obviously lives on. One day near where I live, I saw that someone had painted HH and 88 on the posts around the ice rink there. HH, or the number 88, is one of the symbols most used by neo-Nazis. H is the eighth letter in the alphabet, and the abbreviation stands for Heil Hitler. It may be easy to paint over the graffiti and move on, assuming that a confused youth was behind it. However, three and a half years after a right-wing extremist last arrived on the island, seeing this manifestation of hate here again came as a shock to us all.

Putting aside political dividing lines, conflicts, and civic debates, we must all agree on one thing at least: that we have zero tolerance for fascism and Nazism. These ideologies spread hate—racism, homophobia, misogyny, and hatred of the mentally ill and people with disabilities. We cannot meet this with love, tolerance, openness, and understanding. Tolerance has no place here.

Although the perpetrator has been sent to prison, hate continues to grow both in Norway and the rest of the world. In recent years we have witnessed several hundred neo-Nazis marching through the streets of various Norwegian towns, wearing uniforms and waving flags. In its threat assessment for 2020, the Norwegian Police Security Service considered that right-wing extremists were just as likely to commit an act of terror in Norway as Islamic extremists. These past years have seen the hard right carry out attacks on minorities, religious communities, and political opponents worldwide. In the United States they uncover Far Right terror plots on a monthly basis, while German security services have registered a record number of right-wing extremists. On April 9, 2019, the same day as Nazi Germany invaded Norway in 1940, neo-Nazis hung up banners with swastikas on them in several places proclaiming "We're back." Some Nazis formally join organizations, meet face-to-face, and recruit new members by means of demonstrations, flyers, and stands. Others lurk in the dark corners of the internet. The twenty-one-year-old Norwegian Philip Manshaus murdered his own little stepsister because she wasn't white. He then went to a local mosque in Bærum to kill as many Muslims as possible. Fortunately, his attack on the mosque was a failure. His overall aim was to start a race war. His role model was the man who massacred fifty-one people in an attack on a mosque in New Zealand in March 2019. At the same time he wanted to be sworn in as a member of a neo-Nazi organization called the Nordic Resistance Movement. Internationally we see that a number of terrorists have inspired each other via these channels. The man behind the attack in New Zealand also emulated Breivik. The wave of terror spread from Norway. The Norwegian terrorist's goal was to inspire others, and he has certainly succeeded in doing so. The terror attacks of July 22 could have been a major setback for the Far Right in Norway and the rest of Europe. There was widespread consensus that hate had to be defeated. Today, however, there is very little to suggest that this response has had any effect. As journalist Harald Klungtveit describes in his book *Nynazister blant oss* (Neo-Nazis among is): "As the terrorist attack in Bærum demonstrates, whether the most dangerous neo-Nazis belong to an organization or not is just a matter of chance. It shows how fast radicalization can happen when there is a range of right-wing extremist groups to choose from."

It would be natural to use Utøya to combat Far Right hatred, but would it be the right thing to do? Radicalization and extremism exist in other ideologies too. And the youth is most susceptible to this. We could have chosen a different course, with a more limited impact. We could have chosen to focus on the hate that devastated Utøya. However, an essential component in the prevention of all kinds of extremism, radicalization, and antidemocratic development involves not only fighting these tendencies but also building competence: democratic competence in the younger generation.

I was born in 1984 and grew up in the wake of the fall of the Berlin Wall. When communism and the Soviet Union collapsed, millions of people won their freedom. Democracy as a form of government was gaining ground. More and more countries were becoming democratic. People, ideas, and different media were crossing borders at an ever-increasing rate. The generation that grew up in the 1990s was naïve and optimistic. The world would only get better, almost of its own accord.

But there wasn't only progress in the world. The Chinese authorities brutally cracked down on prodemocracy protests in Tiananmen Square in Beijing. Nationalist extremists set fire to the Balkans and embarked on the ethnic cleansing of minorities. Hutu extremists massacred over eight hundred thousand Tutsis and moderate Hutus in Rwanda. Then four planes were hijacked in the United States, and two of them crashed into the World Trade Center in New York. The world would never be the same again. In recent years, societies we thought were heading steadily in the right direction have been shaken by antidemocratic populists in national assemblies and presidential palaces; human rights are under attack in many parts of the world; the superpower rivalry between the United States and China is constantly reaching new heights; the poverty gap is increasing in and between a considerable number of countries. And in 2022 a full-scale war broke out in Europe. The kind of war we thought we would never see again. A war with terror bombing, thousands of civilian deaths, and several million people driven from their homes.

Civilization has always evolved in fits and starts, but it seems as though we forget that all advances are reversible. The world isn't only going forward. We will keep experiencing setbacks. That is why we must fight for progress. It doesn't come by itself, and nor will it endure without our help. There's nothing natural about a liberal international order. History never came to an end, to paraphrase the political scientist Francis Fukuyama's famous words. Authoritarian forces continued, and still continue, to fight against democracy and liberal values. The institutions that we have based our society on seem much more fragile now than I thought they were in my early adulthood.

Russia's full-scale invasion of Ukraine on February 24, 2022, was not just an immoral war of aggression that breached international law. It was a war against democracy. A totalitarian Russia with Putin at the helm poses a huge threat to both Ukraine and our democratic values. Yet we mustn't forget that even democracies are fully capable of destroying themselves. We mustn't forget to fight the battle that is fought without weapons within Western democracies. It's a matter of democratic readiness, historical awareness, and more critical thinking. The decline of democracies and rise of autocracies should concern us deeply. Political scientific research reveals that many countries that had been developing in a positive direction have become increasingly authoritarian in recent years. This applies to countries all over the world: Turkey, Hungary, Poland, India, Brazil, the United States, the Philippines, Serbia. Because populations can be manipulated, tyrants simply wait for their chance to strike, as history has clearly shown. Antidemocrats often win elections in more or less democratic systems— with promises that their country will become "great again," by telling citizens that they represent "the true people." Antidemocratic populists tell outrageous lies. They meddle with institutions, appoint their own people to key positions, alter electoral systems. Things go pretty much downhill from then on. Antidemocrats know that as long as the lies are big enough and repeated enough times, the democratic debate will be thrown into confusion and derailed. As Filipino journalist and Nobel Laureate Maria Ressa put it: "Without facts, there's no truth. Without truth, there's no trust. Without trust, there's no shared reality, no democracy, and no prospect of tackling the existential problems that the world is facing today."

It is particularly dangerous when the extreme becomes normalized. When words diminish the human value of those whose beliefs, ideas, or looks are not mainstream, people begin to lose sight of the humanity in others. It makes it easier to hate one another. This doesn't happen overnight. It takes some time. The extreme becomes normal. The most important thing we can do happens before violence strikes: we must manage to stop hate from growing and taking root.

Having arenas for peaceful dialogue is key here. For us at Utøya, therefore, reopening the island as a democratic meeting place and center for learning has also meant working to strengthen the sustainability of our society. By facilitating engaging activities inside Hegnhuset, right outside the bullet holes and visible traces of terror in the Cafeteria building, discussions about democratic culture will be strengthened in a completely different way than if they took place elsewhere. The fact that we arrange learning activities for teenagers precisely here, enabling conversations about what democracy means to them, what threatens democracy and how they themselves as citizens can promote democracy in their everyday lives, demonstrates how Utøya can play a central role for all kinds of young people.

A society cannot achieve a democratic culture by simply passing laws in its national assembly. Democracy is a continual process in need of constant safeguarding. Democratic competence must be learned, tested, and put into practice. If young people develop tools for critical thinking, information evaluation, democratic dialogue, and accepting disagreement, they will be well equipped for the rest of their lives. Acknowledging that our world is complex is in itself a rejection of extremist and antidemocratic ideologies, which only promote simplified, black and white worldviews. Working to strengthen democracy is a demanding, long-term project without any immediate results. The core value in a democracy is the participation of citizens in public life. It's only in situations where there is full freedom of speech and information that all citizens can exercise their right to freely express their views, make an informed choice when electing their leaders, and participate actively in the public debate.

Thus liberal democracies cannot be taken for granted. In the history of the world, they are the exception rather than the rule. They can be destroyed from without or within. It is more important than ever before to defend, discuss, and improve liberal democracy.

So remember: democracy comes first, and then everything else comes afterward.

In recent years we have built up a thriving democracy project for the youth, both nationally and internationally. Much of the year Hegnhuset is now filled with teachers, secondary school students, and a number of other groups of young people from Norway and abroad. They read the text messages on the timeline and experience the Cafeteria building close up. They learn about the atrocity that took place here, commemorate the victims, and then proceed to discuss how they themselves can contribute to a tolerant, democratic society, a society that tackles right-wing extremism. They play soccer, buy ice creams at the kiosk, or go for romantic walks along the Path of Love. Commemoration, learning, and engagement in practice.

Our biggest school project lasts for three days. Students learn about the terrorist attacks of July 22, 2011, including their causes and consequences, by means of tasks and visits to the exhibitions and memorial. They also meet witnesses who tell the students their own stories from July 22. With these impressions fresh in their minds and Utøya as the context, the remaining sessions focus on what the students themselves can do as democratic citizens to defend and strengthen our democracy. In parallel with these student activities, their educators learn how to teach controversial topics and facilitate inclusive discussions and debates in the classroom. On the third and final day, the participants plan what to do when they get back home.

The project is available to all Norwegian secondary schools. In the course of these three days, students are free to laugh, cry, play soccer, strengthen their commitment, work to promote democracy and equality, make new friends, and learn about July 22 and those who were impacted by the attacks. Including the subsequent student-run activities held at schools afterward, about ten thousand students benefit from this educational opportunity in Norway each year.

Another of our projects is based on long conversations with Beate Vatndal, mother of Ruth Benedichte Vatndal Nilsen. Year after year I have visited the meetings arranged by the Vestfold support group on the island of Tjøme, and hour after hour I have spoken to Beate about almost everything under the sun, including, of course, Benedichte. When Benedichte was five years old she was diagnosed with Asperger's. As she grew older she was never afraid of standing out or doing her own thing. Benedichte was looking forward to starting upper secondary school, where she would specialize in design, arts, and crafts. She was passionate about "nerd culture" and determined to work as a video game designer. In memory of Benny, and in order to reach out to a broader, more diverse group of young people, this project aims to recruit youngsters from gaming communities in Norway. By learning about, discussing, and reflecting on coding, video game design, and ethics, plus the themes and mechanics used in games, we hope that the younger generation will strengthen their democratic competencies. Although Benedichte was deprived of the possibility to fight for diversity and inclusion after July 22, what she stood for will live on.

Antidemocratic forces and extremism are global threats, however. That is why there's a need for sharing experiences across borders. By exchanging stories, experiences, and practical knowledge, young people become better equipped to withstand extremism and defend the fundamental rights that are important for our society.

One of our international projects is called the Thorvald Stoltenberg seminar. As a former minister of defense, minister of foreign affairs, and diplomat, Thorvald Stoltenberg was a pioneer for Norwegian peace diplomacy. He put great store in dialogue, as exemplified by his informal "breakfast meetings," when he would invite heads of state and foreign ministers to his home for a quiet talk over a cup of coffee at his kitchen table. Thorvald Stoltenberg died in July 2018, and each year a seminar is held in his memory on Utøya. Our aim is to create an arena where young people can learn about and discuss societal challenges while sharing experiences and ideas about how they together and in their respective home countries can contribute to conflict resolution, dialogue, and cooperation.

The Thorvald Stoltenberg seminar lasts five days and brings together participants from Europe and Northern Africa and the Middle East. The young people who attend are engaged in projects supervising youth activities in their homeland. The seminar is arranged and run by international experts with a long record of teaching human rights, global citizenship, and intercultural understanding. We use Utøya as an arena to bring the different participants together. Here they can listen to one other's experiences, discuss possibilities and challenges, and explore how prejudice, hate speech, discrimination, and historical injustice work—with the goal of finding solutions to combat all of this. We must remember that not all polarization is bad, that not all strong disagreements and entrenched debates are harmful. Quite the contrary, such things are a sign that people are unique individuals and that we all help to inform and maintain our democracy. The project has a practical approach, meaning that attendees are introduced to specific tools with which to fight discrimination, facilitate intercultural dialogue, and promote inclusion, as a means of preventing conflicts in their own local and national context.

In order to prevent extremism, probably the most important thing we can do at Utøya and as a society is to strengthen our efforts to develop good, safe, inclusive communities for all of us. At a time of increasing antidemocratic sentiment in Europe and elsewhere, there are still a lot of constructive projects going on involving individuals, organizations, and local communities. We organize a range of different gatherings aimed at highlighting these good examples and supporting positive initiatives to counter attacks on democratic values and institutions.

Another annual project gathers youth politicians and youth activists from Poland, Hungary, the Czech Republic, Slovakia, and Norway for a weeklong democracy workshop at Utøya. Europe today continues to suffer from an economic downturn and social unrest, which in turn serve to exacerbate frustrations as well as politically motivated violence. Extremism takes root and flourishes wherever enough people feel that the political system has failed to solve day-to-day problems. In Poland there is an upsurge of homophobia and xenophobia, and women's rights are being curtailed. Civil society is under attack in Hungary; democracy is under considerable pressure.

In a time of terrorism, extremism, and totalitarianism, the various threats are indistinguishable from each other. It's the same antidemocratic forces that have violated peace so many places around the world. They say they stand for opposing views, but their hate is instantly recognizable. They put themselves above the law. They use violence and kill innocent people. They believe in hate and conspiracy theories. Because the threat is ultimately the same, we must also stand together to fight it.

Democratic peace theory holds that democracy provides an effective protection against war and conflict. Democracies don't go to war with each other and—with some exceptions—don't go to war at all. Democratic development is therefore a development toward peace.

"The situation in Libya is critical, but now it's our responsibility to grasp any glimpse of hope," Mohamed Hamuda told me at Utøya in August 2022. The spokesman for Libya's interim Government of National Unity sat with me under the island's birch trees. We had brought together representatives of Libya's rival governments and groups for closed peace talks. We from Utøya had been working with the peace activist Hajer Sharief and her organization Together We Build It for a year and a half to make these peace talks happen. The meetings were difficult but very constructive. Our objective was to stop the civil war from flaring up again. Although the Utøya initiative lacked the formal status of peace negotiations, eleven central politicians, advisers, and activists from all the most important factions in the war-torn country took part.

The situation in Libya is extremely complex. It would have been dangerous and virtually impossible to gather a group of people like this anywhere in that polarized country. Our initiative managed to bring together a large number of individuals who are active in the peace process. "Utøya is a fantastic place for political discussions," said Wafia Saifalnasr, adviser to Libya's Presidential Council.

After more than ten years of war and conflict, the country is marked by superpower rivalry, foreign mercenaries, rebel fighters, and large-scale human trafficking. Many people felt that all the peaceful alternatives were used up. Our initiative for dialogue at Utøya was therefore all the more important. But, of course, it's not just a matter of sitting down and deciding to achieve peace. It has been our ambition to bring the parties together for honest discussions. We must find the strength to have those painful and difficult conversations. This requires extra courage when things are at their bleakest. And even though the talks were tough, Libya's rival factions were able to speak, sing, and play table tennis together on our green island in the Tyrifjord.

Dialogue is not about forgiveness, forgetting, or excusing others. Dialogue is about listening, trying to understand why and how. It all starts with the words we use. The words we use mean something. Words can divide or unite. Words can break down or build up. Words can hate or create love. Engaging in dialogue is a time-consuming process that cannot be rushed. This is particularly true of dialogues between groups with a wide range of ethical principles and opinions. Yet we also know how valuable such work is, for the parties involved, for individuals, for individual projects—like Utøya—but also for society as a whole, whether it's in Libya or Norway.

For many decades, we have lived in a period of progress tinged with a sad historical legacy that we thought would keep our own continent safe forever. But is our moral compass steady enough when we feel that the kind of life we lead is coming under attack? Are we really so different from those who lived before us?

Our challenge from Utøya is to remember what Martin Luther King Jr. once said: "Darkness cannot drive out darkness; only light can do that. Hate cannot drive out hate; only love can do that."

We must have faith in dialogue. We must ensure that hope is stronger than fear, that love is stronger than hate.

And the most powerful weapon we have is to sit down and talk to each other.

Epilogue

At the time of writing, over six years have passed since Hegnhuset opened and thus six years since the rebuilding of Utøya was completed. It's more than ten years since I was first taken on to work with the island. What I was originally hired to do—help the AUF return to Utøya and at the same time create a meaningful place for those affected and future generations—is in many ways accomplished. The subsequent period has also been challenging, yet very inspiring.

Alice Greenwald, who was responsible for establishing the 9/11 Memorial and Museum in New York, compared the different phases of such work to a birth: it's tough being pregnant, but the real work doesn't begin until the baby comes.

My days still begin with the same drive over Sollihøgda. Jon is still there to meet me at the quay, and the MS *Thorbjørn* still ferries us the six hundred meters or so across to Utøya. Soon there won't be any smell or sound from the diesel engines on board, however, as we are about to replace them with batteries. This old motor landing craft, used by the military and built at the Oskarshamn shipyard on the east coast of Sweden in 1948, is going green. No emissions, no noise to disturb the neighbors, no exhaust fumes from this icon filling Jon's or any other skipper's lungs in the future.

I go aboard the MS *Thorbjørn*, and we cast off from the quay and chug slowly across the water. As the boat sails further into the Tyrifjord, we see the sun emerging from behind the hills in the east. Sunrays light up the highest part of the island, then the hillside, then the Main Building. Then the sun shines through the window of the boat, gradually warming our faces and the cockpit. Jon turns the wheel, changing the angle slightly to avoid getting the sun in his eyes. The bow ramp hits the ground, and we are wedged between the breakwaters. The rope is attached, the engine switched off. We go ashore, walk up the slope, and enter Hovedhuset.

The glass in the old doors between the rooms on the ground floor of the Main Building used to have crusader motifs: crosses, armor, and other symbols. Many of these were what the terrorist used in his manifesto, his propaganda. Several of the panes were broken and needed mending. Should we have them replaced with the same crusader motifs in order to preserve the original design, or should we get rid of these symbols? Breivik saw himself as a modern-day Christian Crusader. We thus decided to replace them with plain glass. Crusaders were no longer welcome here. Upstairs there are two bedrooms and an old disused kitchen. One of the rooms is Jon's. The other used to be a kind of sitting room, where the Utøya staff and AUF leadership could relax during the camp. It opened out onto a balcony. The AUF has traditionally held a camp lunch on the balcony for the AUF and Labor Party leaderships. It was in this room that the perpetrator was questioned straight after he was arrested. The only picture taken after his arrest was of him sitting here on a chair, in handcuffs. Those with a special interest in July 22—police officers and researchers but also a number of ordinary people—often ask about this room. It became clear to me that this should not become "the Breivik room." I therefore took the initiative to remove such associations by making it into a bedroom. At the time, the walls were still covered in that brown paneling that was so popular in the 1970s. We painted the room, then we replaced the windows and laid a new floor. This is now where I sleep when I need to spend the night on the island. It's a bedroom, not an interrogation room.

I leave the Main Building, walk around the corner of the renovated Storehouse, past the Barn and up the hillside. It's now some years since the AUF arranged its first camp here after July 22, but the deafening roar from the twelve hundred enthusiastic campers in 2015 still resounds in the area. Ever since then, one youth organization after the other has done the same thing. We now have motivated campers from a wide range of youth organizations. The AUF still has one thousand young people a year attending its summer camps. More teenagers come to visit the island these days without tents, too. The Ministry of Education and Research finances projects enabling hundreds of secondary school students from all over the country to come to Utøya to learn, commemorate, and get involved.

Back in September 2012 we received a letter from a group of the bereaved demanding that Utøya should become a conservation area. If you only read the newspaper headlines at the time, which many of course did, their demands seemed totally unacceptable. They insisted that the AUF should never again arrange a camp on Utøya and that the whole island should be preserved as it was in the summer of 2011. However, as is the case with most of the conversations we have had with bereaved families and survivors, experts and others, the most interesting part always lies in the details. Among other things the letter states that "the degree of authenticity is of great importance for its value as a historical source." Today we could have written these words ourselves, but it took us some years to understand what they really meant. The letter stressed the need to discontinue all camping activity and focus instead on commemoration and learning. We never agreed on this last point. It was essential for us that all three words be included: commemoration, learning, and engagement. Yet the rest of this letter sent by a number of the bereaved in 2012 provided important input that actually contributed to Utøya's future. I have been in constant dialogue with the initiators of this letter ever since, and over the years I have often taken it out to read it through again.

"Having visited communities and places all over the world that have been targeted by terrorists, the French authorities are convinced that Utøya in Norway is the most impressive," said the French representative during a meeting of the UN in the autumn of 2020.

Today we are contacted by a range of different actors wanting to learn from our process at Utøya. We have been invited to collaborate with a number of national and international organizations.

A tiny little organization like Utøya, a youth organization like the AUF who are themselves victims, how could we have managed to become a world-leading example in how we have dealt with being struck by terror, as Cliff Chanin of the 9/11 Memorial and Museum put it?

I think that one of the main reasons why the Utøya project is now considered relatively successful is that we welcomed external and internal opposition with open arms. Good ideas require an element of doubt. Acknowledging mistakes is essential for development. Listening is the first step in learning. A lot of things have obviously gone wrong. The project was certainly off balance in the beginning. But our work would never have turned out as well as it has without this friction being an integrated part of the process.

As we passed the tenth anniversary of July 22, the government had still not raised a single permanent memorial. There was a court case about one of the two planned memorials, while the other one in the government quarter won't be finished for years. There's still a big discussion about how to incorporate the permanent July 22 Center into the new government building complex. The government has access to all the experts, directorates, and money it needs. Even so, it has got it wrong time after time.

We can all create projects that allow for adjustments at some point, that allow for input from a number of interest groups and others concerned. Yet projects aren't really any good until we are ready to handle disagreements. The fact that we have welcomed criticism, discussion, and debate has been decisive for our work on Utøya these past ten years. Such factors are decisive for a well-functioning democratic society too, as democracy *is* precisely the willingness to compromise, to find common ground when people disagree.

The Cafeteria in many ways became the symbol of how we handled things on Utøya. A lot of people warned us that this building would put an end to the activities outside it. Most AUF members, both old and new, long believed that it wouldn't be possible to combine camping with an intact Cafeteria building. Even with Hegnhuset's new façade, even with the moving symbolism of its posts and pillars, many people thought that the solemnity of the Cafeteria was incompatible with the smiling faces at the campground next door. Because I had never been to an AUF camp and therefore hadn't necessarily understood the dynamics of the campground and the role it played, I simply listened to this kind of feedback. Yet at the same time we had no choice. We couldn't pull down the whole building; we couldn't keep it all either. The July 22 Center was initially located on the ground floor of the high-rise office building in the government quarter, the area most visibly damaged by the explosion. In Hegnhuset the story of July 22 is told in the preserved parts of the Cafeteria building. It was not a foregone conclusion that the Cafeteria and Høyblokken (as the office building is called) would be preserved, and these buildings were certainly not envisaged as places of remembrance and learning. Today we know that it was right to use them. Having a memorial and learning center where terror actually struck is key. It documents the attack, and it creates an authenticity and closeness.

It is also important that Hegnhuset has concentrated July 22 in one building, leaving the other places around the island to live on without that day's tragic events totally dominating the narrative. There is room for the darkness on Utøya, but it has not been allowed to completely obscure the light. This has meant that the entire island can be used, and by many different groups. Youth councils, youth clubs, and youth organizations from Norway and abroad. The AUF on a national and local level. The support group, those affected by July 22, survivors, and the bereaved. This semitransparent Hegnhuset, with its huge glass panels, the placement of its columns, the light streaming in through the screen of posts outside. These details have been decisive for a successful transition between the bustle of life at the campground and the solemn gloom of the Cafeteria. The preserved parts of the Cafeteria building and the open, light, engaging learning arena below create a balanced whole. In this way, one and the same building meets not only the need to remember what happened here and those it affected but also the need for new life and activity.

When we planned and finally built Hegnhuset in 2016, we believed it would be a major contribution to contemporary society and to the future. Without history we lose our way. A lot of art and architecture critics, historians, and commentators from around the world apparently share this view of Hegnhuset.

This same year, the Guardian in the UK described Hegnhuset as one of the top ten new buildings in the world, saying: "A rare example of a memorial site of a terrorist attack handled without mawkish schmaltz or lurid sensationalism, the Hegnhuset on the island of Utøya makes a simple, powerful record of an event that shook the very foundations of Norway's national identity. The café building, where Anders Breivik murdered 13 students, has been retained as a stark relic, its walls sliced with Matta-Clark rawness, and encased in a simple timber and glass pavilion."

The following year Hegnhuset was voted the best educational building in the world. Nevertheless, what matters most to us is that the young people who use the building feel the same way. And we can see that they do. A democracy workshop in practice. That is why Hegnhuset is so important.

I leave Hegnhuset. When the Cafeteria stood here alone, you could see and interpret what had happened in the building just from the bullet holes. Now these bullet holes are contextualized, surrounded by a democracy workshop. The beautiful and moving Memory Book introduces you to the victims. You can read harrowing text messages and see with your own eyes the brutal reality of the great hall. At the same time, you understand the importance of fighting for more tolerance and diversity.

You might think that this unique setting would paralyze visitors, make them passive, but this is where their energy and engagement are most apparent. We dare to talk about the difficult things. This has done something to the atmosphere of the whole island. A major transformation has occurred. It has gone from being a place that only dwelled on the past in the years following 2011 to one that also focuses on the future. It is a significant change.

Right next to Hegnhuset lies our new conference center. This is the de facto heart of Utøya now. This building has followed us on our whole journey since the first plans were presented in 2012. Although it is smaller, situated further north, and simpler than how it was originally conceived, the architectural expression and purpose of the building remain more or less unchanged. This is where we have our meeting rooms, toilets, and dining hall. It's all wood, glass, and concrete—modern Norwegian design. When you walk down the corridor you can see what is happening outdoors, too. It's transparent and open, so you see the natural surroundings through the enormous windows. The rooms are large and light, with high ceilings. The oppressive, claustrophobic feeling you might experience in the Cafeteria building disappears in this airy, spacious conference center. Here you can relax and find peace of mind after the challenges of Hegnhuset.

Visiting Utøya is both pleasant and painful; this is only natural. And this is how it will remain, too. Because July 22, 2011, has become part of the island's unique history. The special circumstances mean that time spent on Utøya is different than anywhere else, since our visitors' mental and physical presence here strengthens the value of the social and academic content. Organizations such as Amnesty International have no direct connection to Utøya, the labor movement, or July 22. But discussing how to fight for, further develop, and improve the work for human rights and equality feels particularly right and relevant here. Therefore courses and meetings for volunteer organizations and associations involved with solidarity, law, emergency preparedness, or youth engagement fill our premises for much of the year.

When we otherwise use names like the Path of Love, Bolshevik Cove, Stoltenberget, and the Bay of Pigs, calling our new conference center Torget, meaning a town or village square, wasn't exactly inspired. I will leave the task of changing this name to future generations. We have already named some of its rooms, though. The conference hall is called "Gro" after Gro Harlem Brundtland, the so-called Queen of Utøya. Gro was the last guest to deliver a major speech on Utøya in 2011 and the first to deliver a major speech here in 2015. One of the meeting rooms has been called "Palme" in memory of the assassinated Swedish prime minister. This is a way of thanking our Swedish friends, particularly the SSU (the AUF's sister organization in Sweden), which gave 5 million kroner and a great deal of moral support and assistance to our efforts to rebuild Utøya.

The last name has also been the most important one: "Café Monica." Monica, who was so dear to Jon and their daughters Victoria and Helene. So dear to the AUF and Utøya. It's the dining hall that is called after Monica. A place for tasty meals and interesting conversations. The stories about Monica live on through all the guests who haven't been here before but who wonder who has given the room its name.

In the library, five meter high bookshelves cover one of the walls. Through the huge expanses of glass you can see the Tyrifjord, the sunset, the snow-capped mountaintops of Norefjell, and the farmlands of Røyse. In one corner there's a self-service, alcohol-free bar. In another there's a well-used black Fender, of the type favored by Jimi Hendrix, George Harrison, and Kurt Cobain. And Torjus Jakobsen Blattmann. We have been given the guitar, amplifier, and other equipment by Trond and Mette, Torjus's parents. He was passionate about music and a skilled guitar player. He used to spend much of his time practicing in the rock tent during the summer camps on Utøya. Torjus and several other teenagers who died were supposed to be giving a concert from the stage on Saturday, July 23. It means a lot to his parents that Torjus's guitar can still bring music, joy, and that distinctive "fuzz" sound to the island that Torjus loved so much.

I stroll across the square outside Torget, under the NATO sign by the corner of the Gro conference hall, and along the path heading north to the Clearing. With a microfiber cloth in one hand, I wipe over the metal ring of names. I remove a couple of withered flowers. The cables hanging from the pine trees are nice and taut.

When the memorial was finished in 2015, it only had sixty out of the sixty-nine names. Nine names were missing. There were various reasons for this. Some families hadn't been able to face making a decision about using their deceased child's name, some wouldn't agree until they saw how the memorial, and Utøya in general, actually turned out, while others refused to give their permission as a kind of protest against the direction Utøya had taken. Since 2015 I have basically been in constant dialogue with the families who didn't give their permission at the time. The following year, five families got in touch to say that they now wanted the names of their loved ones inscribed on the ring. We therefore carefully dismantled it. To avoid damaging the roots of the pines in the Clearing, no heavy machinery is allowed in the area between the trees, so once again we had to lift almost a ton of steel manually. A new section of names was produced and the ring reassembled. The entire process took a couple of weeks and cost tens of thousands of kroner. The important thing was that the families had taken the time they needed, that the names were added when the families themselves were ready. In 2018 the same process happened again with the last four names. Having them all means a lot to us and to the memorial. Now sixty-nine names shimmer from the ring in the glade.

My calendar still contains the tributes to each of the victims on their birthdays. Sixty-nine birthdays, sixty-nine days that are especially important to remember. On every birthday, one of us working at Utøya walks over to the memorial. We take a flower that we have picked somewhere on the island. We hang it nicely from the person's name, so all our guests can pay their respects to this person in particular. It is another occasion to honor a life, to remember a person who is no longer with us. For those of us who work here, it is also a valuable reminder of the legacy bestowed on us.

There are often a few flowers missing from the ground around the glade. It's easy to point the finger at our goats, but they usually prefer buds, thorns, and bark. After each visit, there are always guests who have picked flowers from the surrounding woodland and placed them in the names on the ring. Very few of our visitors actually knew any of the victims, yet many people appreciate being allowed to hang flowers from the names. Seeing these names every day is a good reminder, a good occasion to think about all of those who are still sorely missed by so many nationwide.

"How long does it take to walk around the whole island?" is a question we are often asked. The answer seems to be a whole book. Just as a stroll around the island can take varying amounts of time; this book could also have been considerably longer. There are far more stories from the old days, far more descriptions of the inconceivable fear and suffering from 2011, far more conversations with the bereaved, survivors, and other people affected.

When the day's work is done, we go down to MS *Thorbjørn* to be ferried back to the mainland. As the boat turns in the water and heads away from Utøya, I often find myself taking pictures of the island's characteristic silhouette—as if I didn't have enough identical photos on my phone already. But deep down I think that something is telling me I am only here on a visit. Just as other guests take pictures when they leave, so do I. It is of course my island too at the moment, but at the same time I am just a visitor.

I have written this book more ten years after the right-wing extremist attacks targeted Oslo and Utøya in 2011. More or less ten years of my life have passed since it happened. I was twenty-six when I was asked to help out. Utøya has now taken over half my career.

I have had the honor of managing the island through a demanding period of its long history, but at some point everything comes to an end. I will then do something else with my life and let someone else take over the reins—just as many have done before me, and many will do in the future. That is maybe the reason I have hundreds of pictures of Utøya from precisely this angle.

For some years, people called and texted me night and day. It made my private life more challenging and my job more stressful. At the same time, it was also the reason that I couldn't bring myself to quit. I felt that I meant something to others, that I had a positive impact on other people's lives. It was this that kept me going. All the traveling I have done in recent years has given me the chance to get to know the whole country, a variety of people and landscapes. The support groups from the west and north of Norway, for example, have often held their gatherings cruising up the Norwegian coast with Hurtigruten. As a result, several of our meetings and conversations have combined some of the toughest and loveliest things imaginable.

One unforgettable moment was on board one of these ships with the support group from Nordland. One night a couple of us sat in the jacuzzi on deck in the pitch dark talking about everything under the sun. But mostly about Utøya, of course, about July 22 and its aftermath. In the middle of a conversation about what it was like to go on living without this precious person family member, how hard it was to keep being reminded of how he was killed, the sky turned from black to green. A magnificent display of northern lights danced across the heavens. Fighting back my tears of joy and pain, I was glad that it was both dark and wet in the jacuzzi—as a young father, a fellow human, and the one in charge of Utøya.

Having worked so closely with Utøya and those concerned by July 22 for so many years, it's natural to wonder if we have become hardened and slightly cynical. A lot of people ask my colleagues and myself about this. "Does what happened here still affect you when you're surrounded by it every day?" Working on the Memory Book, for example, during the spring and summer of 2019 made it clear that we definitely still had feelings. All around me were pictures and texts about young people that I had come to know very well since their deaths, and I now knew most of their parents too. We cried each day while we made the book.

My job has been, and still is, incredibly rewarding—making this place as meaningful as possible for the years to come, for thousands of youngsters from around the world, for the bereaved and the survivors. You don't need to spend a long time with motivated teenagers before you feel reenergized.

However terrible and traumatic the massacre was, the sun *will* always shine again. It is both comforting and painful to remember this. In his speech at the final commemoration ceremony in Oslo in August 2011, Jens Stoltenberg gave the nation three tasks: see who was affected, fight hate with arguments, and bring back security. He also urged us to take responsibility, guard our freedom, and together forge unbreakable links of compassion, democracy, and safety. We have put these words into action on Utøya. Most people thought it was an impossible challenge. But as Nelson Mandela so aptly put it: "It always seems impossible until it's done."

Thousands of people now visit Utøya every year, both from Norway and abroad. They learn about what happened on that darkest of days, and about the importance of the fight against extremism, fascism, and xenophobia. They come to a gathering point and political workshop for engaged youth, a place for culture, sport, friendship, and love. They come to a place that has the memory of those we lost on July 22 in its heart, a place that never forgets, a place where new generations can uphold the ideals that were attacked. They come here to meet others, remember, discuss, reflect, agree, disagree, think critically, and think big. They come here to create a society where we can live together in harmony, free to express our opinions. A society where we see differences as opportunities, where hope is stronger than fear.

Here on Utøya we have chosen to continue walking on the Path of Love. Because love will conquer hate—but only if we stand up for tolerance and against xenophobia. It's up to me, and it's up to you. Every single day.

Utøya's light did not go out. Utøya stood firm. Together we have created a story of hope, not fear. Fellowship, not division. Light, not darkness. A story of love and dialogue.

On MS *Thorbjørn*'s bow ramp we have written the last line of Frode Grytten's poem from July 2011. For me it sums up what this little island in the Tyrifjord is all about:

hey, hey, time to get up and change the world

Acknowledgments

Utøya would not be what it is today without the help of thousands of people. I would like to thank all of you who have contributed to this important undertaking.

The biggest thanks I can give go to all those affected—the bereaved and the survivors—who in the midst of their grief opened their homes to us, invited us in to discuss Utøya's future, and provided constructive input. It's because of you that Utøya has become such an important place—for the families, for the AUF, and for Norway.

Thanks to all of you who were initially critical of the project but have subsequently proved vital in helping to make Utøya what it is today. And thank you to all the enthusiasts who never lost sight of the goal, even when others doubted that we could accomplish our objective.

With so many people involved—from all walks of life, from Norway and abroad, a range of ages, with very different connections to the island and with various political allegiances—it would have been unreasonable to expect that the process would be painless. Pain is one of the most fundamental human experiences. For me personally, experiencing, hearing about, and sharing so much pain has not been natural. Not so much pain, so often, and for so long. Yet we have also found the energy and drive in this pain to fight for important but challenging projects. The close contact I have had with so many lovely people has meant a lot to me. Bereaved families send me flowers on my birthday, and I receive thoughtful Christmas greetings from a number of them each year. My children have been given presents: hand-knitted mittens, sweaters, and homemade bags. I have become close with many of the parents who were the most difficult to deal with in the beginning. Thanks for letting us get to know you.

A huge thank you to the national support group, which represents a great diversity of opinions on what should happen to Utøya, and which under Trond and Lisbeth's leadership has managed to balance these views in a dignified and respectful way. You have given us sound advice over the years.

Among the bereaved it is my close colleague Jon who deserves the biggest thanks. Until 2017 we were the only ones working on Utøya. While I saw to the process, he saw to the island. This courageous man belongs in a Hollywood film; he's an inspiration to us all. Jon is as solid as they come.

In addition to Jon and others who were affected, there are two men in particular that I talked to day in and day out. In the car, on walks, on trips around the country, on the way to and from soccer practice—there were few opportunities that weren't used to discuss matters on the phone with Tor Einar Fagerland and Jan Christian Vestre.

Tor Einar's advice and input on memorial issues was crucial. He has always seen the process for what it is and where it is and has acted constructively to find solutions throughout. "We are here to keep you company during this incredibly difficult process," Tor Einar would say about the role that he and the resource group played.

Not only as a specialist in his field, but also as a link between us and the international experts, Tor Einar soon became central to this part of the project. I would contribute feedback from the AUF, families, and survivors, plus my own opinions. Tor Einar would digest the material, then discuss it with James Young, Alice Greenwald, and Ed Linenthal. And so the months passed, with discussions back and forth about this and that—but mostly about how to achieve the unique balance we were after. Tor Einar, Ed, James, and Alice all deserve my deepest gratitude.

Most important of all is Jan Christian Vestre. Jan Christian was himself at Utøya on July 22. He was a long-term board member of Utøya and also on AUF's executive board. In 2010 he had led an internal feasibility study for the Workers' Youth League about rehabilitating the island, so he knew the buildings and infrastructure very well. When Martin Henriksen stepped down, it was Jan Christian who took over as chairman. Jan

Christian and I worked very closely together. We had endless discussions about how to solve the problems we faced. We had similar thoughts on a lot of issues, but quite different approaches. We would not have managed to accomplish all we have without the wise and visionary Jan Christian.

The important choices made early on by Eskil Pedersen, Åsmund Aukrust, and Mari Aaby West of the AUF leadership team were crucial. Future generations of AUF youth should be very grateful to these three. They stuck to their decision to rebuild Utøya while also showing a willingness to listen, take their time, and modify the plans.

Next up is Erlend Blakstad Haffner, the architect who skillfully handled one of the most challenging architecture projects imaginable. It has been a difficult process and demanding work for an architect, but Erlend has shown himself to be flexible, pragmatic, and solution oriented—without ever compromising on the required architectonic qualities.

A big thank you to our enthusiastic volunteers, motivated AUF supporters of all ages who have always helped out when needed.

All the thousands of people who visit Utøya often have very different reasons for coming. They may have come in small groups for a guided tour and a lecture about how we manage this special place; they may be at summer camp; they may be secondary school students attending a democracy workshop; or they may be families of the victims who have come to remember their loved ones. All of them will visit the same places, walk along the same road, use the same buildings. It is therefore essential that our facilities function appropriately at all times.

So that each visit feels positive, balanced, meaningful, and memorable—regardless of who is visiting and why—our presence and input are key. We therefore spend a lot of time ensuring that our guests feel the island is run not just sustainably, but with dignity and a personal, loving touch. To achieve this kind of quality, there are several of us on the staff with plenty to do. Lars, Ann Helen, Harald, Silje, Paul, Jane, Ragnar, Anne Britt, and Jon, you are simply the best! We also have lots of great educators, and we collaborate with talented individuals in various organizations. These are dedicated, wonderful people who are always busy doing important things.

My girlfriend has been a vital support to me throughout these ten years of hard work. Mona, my love for you is eternal.

Thanks also to Paul Patrick Børhaug, my good friend, colleague, and traveling companion. Your knowledge of literature, music, photography—and your jokes—brightens up my day. Your backing of this book project has spurred me on. A special mention to Martine Norli Solstad, my dear sister Hilde W. Frydnes, and my friend and colleagues Maja Gudim Burheim and Lars Gudmundson who have provided feedback on the manuscript.

The book *Utøya—en biografi*, written by Jo Stein Moen and Trond Giske in 2012, has been an important source of information about the history of the island.

I could not have written this book without the support of my Norwegian editor Stian Bromark and my American editor Mary Dougherty. Thanks for the useful tips, advice, and follow-up. Your patience and attention to detail have been crucial. Thank you so much!

My final thanks go to all of you that use Utøya every year. Young people from Norway and abroad. You are our hope—you are the future.